Tiger

Animal
Series editor: Jonathan Burt

Already published

Forthcoming

Tiger

Susie Green

REAKTION BOOKS

Dedicated to all those who strive in their different ways to save the wild places of the world from the curse of development

Published by
REAKTION BOOKS LTD
33 Great Sutton Street
London EC1V 0DX, UK

www.reaktionbooks.co.uk

First published 2006
Copyright © Susie Green 2006

Printed in China

British Library Cataloguing in Publication Data
Green, Susie
    Tiger. – (Animal)
    1. *Tigers*
    I. Title
    599.7'56

    ISBN-10: 1 86189 276 4
    ISBN-13: 978 1 86189 276 8

Contents

1 Evolution and Natural History

There is no savage beast in the jungle save that which
has been made savage by man.
Patrick Hanley

As the origins of the world are shrouded in mystery so are those
of the world's supreme predator, the tiger. The Naga of northeast India believe that when the earth was young, the ancient
scaly pangolin, a wondrous anteater, allowed the mother of the
first spirit, the first man and the first tiger to emerge through
his deep burrow onto the verdant earth. The tiger went to dwell
in the dark, luxuriant forests while his brother, being human,
stayed at home. Eventually the man ventured into the forest,
where he was forced to fight his tiger brother, whom he tricked
into crossing a river, then killed with a poisoned dart. The gold-
en-black striated body floated gently on the river's currents and
finally came to rest in a bed of reeds, where it was discovered by
the divine Dingu-Aneni. Realizing the tiger was born of woman
and thus man's brother he took the tiger's bones from the waters
and for ten long years covered them with his warm body until
hundreds of tigers sprang from the bones and populated the
plains and the forests.

The palaeontologists are not certain of what they believe and
are accompanied in their uncertainty by molecular biologists.
As one expert in the field, Alan Turner, wrote at the end of the
twentieth century, 'Despite the outline understanding of felid
evolution that we now have, it should be stressed that we still
lack any clear idea of the immediate ancestry of the living

species or the more precise pattern of relationships between them.'[1]

This, however, is a widely accepted classification:

Kingdom: Animalia
Phylum: Chordata (vertebrates)
Class: Mammalia
Order: Carnivora
Family: Felidae
Sub Family: Machairodontinae, the sabre-toothed cats
    with flattened and elongated canines
Sub Family: Felinae or 'true cats', those with conical
    canines (all the *Panthera*)
Genus: *Panthera*
Species: *Panthera tigris* (the tiger), *Panthera leo* (the lion),
    Panthera pardus (the leopard)

One of the major problems from a palaeontologist's point of view is the lack of fossil remains. Carnivores are massively outnumbered by their prey and comprise a mere 2 per cent of the world's animals. The conditions for fossilization occur rarely, so the chances of felid remains in particular being discovered are extremely rare and the margin for error in tracing lineage large, but despite this, theories, like the carnivores, have evolved.

The general consensus of opinion is that the first creatures we class as Carnivora appeared on the earth during the Palaeocene, some 60 million years ago. These were all-purpose Carnivora, with teeth capable of cracking bones, shearing flesh and grinding. They had claws and could probably climb trees. As the millennia passed, these creatures began to fit into different ecological niches giving rise to more specialized Carnivora until, around 30 million years ago, during the Oligocene, the remains of what we would think of as a cat, *Proailurtus lemanensis*, although with rather more teeth, were deposited in France. Chronologically the next cat, unearthed in New Mexico and California, was a rather puma-like creature, *Pseudaelurus*, whose skeleton suggests she was a fabulous tree climber.

Many people think *Pseudaelurus* was the ancestor of both what we think of as modern cats, from a radiation beginning with *Pseudaelurus schizailurus* around 20 million years ago in the Miocene, and the sabre-toothed cats or machairodonts, of whom there are now no known living examples, from a radiation of the same era.

All modern cats, from tiger to Siamese, posses strong conical canines, ideal for attacking and seizing prey with. This, for many authorities, rules out the sabre-toothed cats as their ancestor as these machairodonts all had extremely long, flat, 'sheared' canines, ideal for slicing through flesh but far too fragile to seize prey with. In short, for many, the sabre-toothed 'tiger' was most certainly *not* a tiger – but there are other, more recent, contenders such as *Dinofelis*, who padded the earth a mere 5 million years ago. Also known as 'false sabre-toothed' tigers because their canines, although partially flattened, were only the length of those of a contemporary tiger, they ranged through North America, Europe, Africa and Asia until perhaps as recently as ten thousand years ago, dining on antelopes, baboons and australopithecines. *Dinofelis abeli* was a giant form that inhabited China, bringing to mind the enormous modern tigers of Manchuria. Hemmer, a renowned German zoologist, is of the opinion that *Panthera* took over *Dinofelis'* ecological niche, and this, combined with recent biomolecular comparisons which reveal the close similarity between the American *Smilodon* (what most people think of as the 'classic'

A group of *Smilodon fatalis*, a Pleistocene-era sabre-toothed cat, hunting a bison.

sabre-toothed tiger), and the modern-day leopard and lion, the other members of the *Panthera* genus, gives rise to an alternative theory, that the sabre-toothed tiger really is *Panthera tigris'* ancestor after all.

There is similar confusion regarding the timing and geographical dispersion of *Panthera tigris*. Hemmer believes there are no undisputed *Panthera* fossil remains in the otherwise well represented carnivore communities of Europe, Africa or North America before the late Pliocene, around 2 million years ago. This suggests that *Panthera tigris* originated in Asia, in all probability east Asia, from whence it spread in two directions: west, over the north central Asian woodlands and river systems, and then south into India; east into the mountains of central Asia, then on to south-east Asia, Burma, Vietnam, and the islands of Indonesia from whence it reached India. The tiger, unlike any other big cat, is an extremely strong swimmer, able to cover many kilometres, allowing her to populate areas out of reach to other *Panthera*.

Other authorities feel that the tiger originated in Siberia and when ice ages made the area inhospitable fanned out south, in search of warmer climes. Sandra Herrington, who has been studying skulls in modern-day Alaska, believes both the lion and tiger were living there within the last 100,000 years and that the tiger, like the lion, crossed the Bering Land Bridge into the Americas during times of lowered sea levels.[2] However, the role of camouflage, often disregarded in palaeontology, is extremely important to a predator such as the tiger, which ambushes its prey. It seems extremely unlikely the tiger would have evolved a coat so fabulously indistinguishable in the broken shadow of elephant grass or forest in the bleak sandy scrublands of northern Russia.

Molecular biologist Stephen O'Brien, using the molecular clock as a dating system, as does Hemmer, believes the *Panthera* separated into separate species around 2 million years ago. However, whereas Hemmer believes that the subspecies of *Panthera tigris* such as the Javan and Manchurian tiger evolved at the same time, O'Brien, whose research reveals that the genetic differences between the modern tiger subspecies is four times less than those between human racial groups, believes that these geographical *Panther tigris* subspecies could only have evolved in the last 10,000 years.

Whichever theory one supports, and there are many more than it is within the scope of this book to cover, what does seem certain is that the earliest indisputable *Panthera tigris* fossils discovered to date come from Yenchinkou, Szechwan, in China and are around 1.5 million years old,[3] and as the tiger is not indigenous to Sri Lanka she must have reached southern India after the watery straits between the subcontinent and Sri Lanka widened beyond even her swimming capacity.

It is also certain that in 1900 there were eight subspecies of tiger:

Caspian Tiger *Panthera tigris virgata*
Vital statistics: Now extinct

Siberian/Amur Tiger *P.t. altaica*
Vital statistics: 400 or less, mainly living in the woodlands of
    eastern Russia.
Male: Length: 3.35 m, weight: 300 kg
Female: Length: up to 2.6 m, weight: 90–170 kg;
    unusually pale orange in colour with black stripes
Main prey: elk and wild boar

South China Tiger *P.t. amoyensis*
Vital statistics: Probably now extinct

Indochinese Tiger *P.t. corbetti*
Vital statistics: reputedly 1,500 mainly living in remote
    forests and hilly terrain in Thailand, southern China, Laos,
    Malaya (discovered 2004), Cambodia and Vietnam.
    (This may be an optimistic estimate: information is
    scarce and no census has been made)
Male: Length: 2.75 m, weight: 180 kg
Female: Length: 2.45 m, weight 114 kg
Main prey: wild pig, wild deer and wild cattle

Bengal Tiger *P.t. tigris*
Vital statistics: perhaps 2,500 and dropping constantly;
    mainly in India with others in Nepal, Bangladesh,
    Bhutan and Myanmar
Male: Length: 2.9 m, weight: 218 kg

Female: Length: 2.44 m, weight: 136 kg
Prey: wild deer and wild cattle

Sumatran Tiger *P.t. sumatrae*
Vital statistics: probably far less than 400 individuals in
    lowland, sub-mountain, mountain and peat-moss forest
Male: Length 2.9 m, weight: 120 kg
Female: Length 2.15 m, weight: 91 kg
Darkest of all the tigers, with broad black stripes and
    striped forelegs
Main prey: wild pig, large deer (rusa) and muntjac deer

Javan Tiger *P.t. sondaica*
Now extinct

Balinese Tiger *P.t. balica*
Now extinct

Besides differing coat markings, there is a huge variation in size between these subspecies, mainly because in hot climates animals usually *decrease* in size (the smaller the animal, the greater the evaporation surface area as a proportion of body weight, allowing more efficient dissipation of heat). However, Baikov and Yankovsky, hunting in Manchuria in the first half of the twentieth century, insist very large and much smaller tigers inhabited the same areas and that they were separate subspecies. As tigers are virtually extinct in the area it is impossible to check this, but Yakovsky claimed that many hundreds of years ago the ancient Mongol emperors designated hundreds of square miles of land north of the Tumen river, quite near what is now Vladivostok, as a sanctuary for tigers and leopards imported from India.[4] Over several centuries evolution, probably combined with

A 15th-century Iranian or Central Asian ink and wash drawing of a tiger.

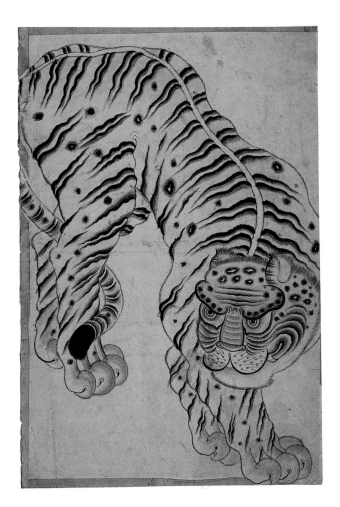

selective culling of small tigers, lead to the emergence of a race of massive tigers possessing heavy, luxuriant, light-coloured coats, and reaching 4.25 m in length and weighing over 250 kg. Eventually, the sanctuary was abandoned and the tigers spread north to Sakhalin island and south to Korea and northern China, where they bred with the local tiger population creating a massive subspecies. Others claim that certain local mineral salts are responsible for the tiger's great growth.[5] Yankovsky killed what was probably the last of these tigers around 1956.

What is known of the natural history of the tiger is inseparable from how she was treated by the prevailing culture of the time and the conditions under which she lived – and that is as true today when she lives in reserves much visited by tourists as it was when the Mughal emperor Jahangir (1568–1616) kept pet tigers in a stupendous menagerie. His observations tell us something of how tigers behave in luxurious captivity and prevailing attitudes of the time.

> As in the time of my reign wild beasts have abandoned their savagery, tigers have become so tame that troops of them without chains or restraint go about amongst the people, and they neither harm men nor have any wildness or alarm. It happened that a tigress became pregnant and after three months bore three cubs; it had never happened that a wild tiger after its capture had paired. It had been heard from great philosophers that the milk of a tigress was of great use for brightening eyes. Although we made every effort that the moisture of the milk should appear in her breasts, we could not accomplish it. It occurs to me that as it is a raging creature, and milk appears in the breasts of mothers by reason of the affection they have for their young, perhaps . . . it dried up because we were not her cubs.

In India, tigresses' milk is still regarded as a wonderful panacea for eye problems but, as the pioneering Indian naturalist Salim

Ali (1896–1987) remarked, 'the difficulty in obtaining it, however, probably has much to do with its reputed efficacy'.

Observations of the tiger during the Raj, when she was hunted ceaselessly and her habitat decimated, tell little of her natural history but something of how a great predator behaves when its entire population is viciously hunted. Much was written of her unnatural history by those whose aim was to shatter her heart or mind with a bullet and to emphasize her viciousness to enhance their valour. One notable exception was Patrick Hanley, a planter and naturalist who lived for 15 years prior to World War II in the fortuitously neglected forests of Assam. Thanks to him we are given a glimpse into a world that reveals something of the tiger's true natural history. Sadly, Hanley's diaries and photographs were mostly burnt during World War II, but in 1961 a book of his memoirs was published. Interestingly, many of his observations on the tiger are similar to those that the naturalist and conservationist Valmik Thapar, who is studying tigers in Ranthambore reserve, are rediscovering in tigers who have never known persecution and its attendant fear.

Hanley had a predilection for gathering jungle orchids on foot, which brought him into close proximity with tigers on an almost daily basis. He knew 60 individuals by sight (every tiger has unique markings), and not one attempted to harm him or even snarled at him. 'I have come across scores of tigers unexpectedly', he wrote. 'Even when they followed me, it was at a respectful distance, and this was done purely out of curiosity, and a desire to see what this strange creature they had never seen before was doing in their preserves.' As he succinctly put it, 'Half the things a man fears in the jungle are imaginary things, he sees himself in untenable positions and he credits the jungle creatures with a savagery which they do not really possess.'

Contemporary wildlife researchers in India who spend much time in the field also come face to face with the striped feline. Shekhar Kolipakar, one of the world's leading small cat experts, was putting up a camera trap at the side of a large pond in Panna Tiger Reserve when he noticed a tigress with a large cub, watching him closely from a few feet away. Kolipakar simply relaxed and stayed where he was. In a moment, curiosity satisfied, mother and son continued their stroll. Three other field researchers at Panna were returning a little drunk from a party through a reserve forest, an area open to anyone but in which it is forbidden to trap, hunt or take wood. One, the worse for wear, sat down, little realizing a tiger was walking straight towards him. In vain his companions, who had gone on ahead not realizing their friend was no longer with them, called and cried, but the tiger continued on. They raced back – their friend was gone. Fearing the worst they frantically searched the nearby bushes where their friend, deeply asleep, alcohol having got the better of him, breathed gently. The tiger's pug marks (paw prints) passed right over his vulnerable body but she had not harmed him in any way.[6]

Tigers are also relaxed when observed by humans on elephant back, even if with their cubs, because they have learnt that the presence of the elephant is a guarantee of their safety, unlike during the Raj, when it was a prelude to death or devastating injury. Nonetheless, tigers, just like humans, have a clearly defined personal space which they object to having invaded, and will deliver a mock charge to make their point.

They also have their moods, easily recognizable to one who studies them. They may be grumpy, amused or angry and, like a domestic cat, need to be treated accordingly. They also have certain instinctive reactions. Flight provokes them to pursue and attack, as it does all predators, including infuriated domestic dogs. This reaction is also stimulated by bending over and, crucially, falling over. For a tiger, groups of humans bending over, for instance to cut grass for fodder, resemble tempting herds of four-legged herbivores. However, tigers virtually always cease to regard humans as prey the moment that they stand upright. This was confirmed by Kailish Sankhala, using the tigers in his charge as subjects, when he was the groundbreaking animal welfare director of Delhi Zoo from 1965 to 1970. The tigress, like all other mothers, defends her cubs fiercely from attack or kidnap, but the reality is that unless particularly provoked, tigresses, like dogs, will merely growl a warning, and the wise will calmly look away and leave slowly.[7]

Man and tiger have always met one another in the jungle but, like all top predators, the tiger chooses on the whole to avoid man, a fact noted over 2,000 years ago by Pliny, who in the eighth book of his *Natural History* writes:

> A tigress it is said, even though savage to all other animals and herself scorning the footprints of even an elephant, when she sees the track of a human being, at once carries her cubs elsewhere – though how has she recognized or where has she seen before the person that she fears? For it is certain that such forests are very little frequented. Granted that no doubt they may be surprised by the mere rarity of the print; but how do they know that it is something to be afraid of? Indeed there is a further point, why should they dread even the sight of man himself when they excel him so greatly in strength, size and speed? Doubtless it is Nature's law and shows her power, that the fiercest and largest wild beasts may never have seen a thing that they ought to fear and yet understand immediately when they have to fear it.[8]

A tiger without stripes, from a 12th-century Latin Bestiary; the accompanying text calls the animal 'speckled'.

This natural desire to avoid man, combined with the almost limitless forest and abundant prey at the forest lord's disposal, meant that until the Raj stepped up its activities around 1800, tigers came into contact with man relatively rarely and generally had neither the need, nor desire, to take his cattle.

Occasionally villagers and those such as the honey harvesters of the Sundarbans, whose way of living still takes them constantly into the tiger's domain, have been attacked and killed in situations where if they had known how to defuse the tiger's aggression, to alter how the tiger perceived them, tragedy might have been avoided. Sometimes this was and still continues to be regarded as a tribute to the forest, sometimes as an unavoidable evil in much the same way as societies dependent upon the car accept the death of thousands of their members as a necessary ill which allows them to maintain a particular lifestyle. Virtually never was the tiger branded as a man-eater.

All that altered with the advent of the British. A campaign of extinction was embarked upon by the upper echelons of the Raj, latterly assisted by the maharajas who butchered India's wildlife in a status-driven frenzy of blood lust. Fanny Eden, the sister of the Governor-General of India, writing in 1835 of

'Bisgaum charges the dying tiger', an illustration from Samuel W. Baker's *Wild Beasts and their Ways* (1890).

a small hunting expedition comprising a mere 260 camp follow-ers and 20 elephants, describes two ladies in the party. 'They regularly get upon their elephants, and go tiger hunting every-day; they talk of the excitement of the tiger's spring and the "excellent day they saw eight killed".' Colonel Rice's proud tally of 93 tigers killed or wounded during four summer vacations was nothing unusual;[9] lifetime tallies of over 1,000 were common.

In 1947 India at last gained its independence. A great day for India's people, a terrible one for the tiger, who was already severely compromised and hovering on the brink of extinction. During the Raj, although the slaughter was massive, it was at least confined to the ruling class. This once exclusive activity was now seized on by the Indian people as a democratizing one, and wholesale extermination began. Amateur hunters, shikar operators (who ran tiger hunting as a package holiday), professional poachers and farmers all joined in. If that were not enough, large-scale hunting campaigns were organized, nets were spread, pits were dug, traps were laid, forests were burned. From well over 100,000 in 1600, around 50,000 in 1900, tiger numbers were reduced to less than 2,500 by 1970.

Bengal tigers simply didn't stand a chance. They were killed while sleeping and while mating, while eating and while stalking; foetuses were taken from the still warm bodies of their mothers to increase bag numbers, and they were unable to escape from the pockets of remaining forest they inhabited. By around 1800, when the slaughter really began to escalate, every tiger that came in contact with man realized that he was their merciless enemy and from that moment their reactions were almost exclusively dominated by fear. Existing in a state of constant tension, their forests disturbed day and night, tormented without cessation, tigers, like people living in a war zone, became more aggressive and in order to avoid their tormentors much more solitary. The forests began to harbour large numbers of wounded tigers in terrible pain. Tigers with their jaws fractured, slowly starving to death; tigers with bullets embedded in their flesh creating poisonous and sometimes gangrenous wounds; tigers with lacerated paws – small wonder they became vicious.

'The End of our Tiger Hunt', from William T. Hornaday's *Two Years in the Jungle* (1885).

Hunters also killed much of the tiger's natural prey, including the nilgai (a large Indian antelope). After independence this slaughter also increased exponentially to cater for city restaurants, where venison suddenly became fashionable. The nilgai too, became an endangered species. The tiger, already reduced to sporadic cattle depredation, now had little option but to take domestic animals to survive. Generously issued with guns and crop protection licences by the government, farmers did not hesitate to kill cubs and tigresses alike.

The tiger's territories were mined, her forests plundered for timber or turned into grazing and arable land. Gradually she was forced into smaller and smaller areas until eventually she only survived in fragmented pockets surrounded by farmland and villages. Conflict was inevitable. The tiger had nowhere to go. Brought unwillingly into constant contact with man, her behaviour inevitably had to change to deal with the utterly unnatural situation she found herself in. To take one instance, the slaughterers of the Raj maintained that the tiger was entirely nocturnal, which no doubt it then was, for two principal reasons:

first an overwhelming fear of man, second because in conditions where prey species are becoming scarce, hunting at night gives an added advantage. However, in the peaceful jungles of Assam, Hanley often saw tigers hunting diurnally, and this behaviour is now observed in protected reserves. The altered environment also affects other creatures' behaviour. For instance in Panna at night many spotted deer, much desired by tiger and leopard, leave the confines of the forest and move close to the villages outside the reserves, because they know tigers avoid human habitation. It is thus more advantageous for the tiger to hunt deer by day, when the deer avoid human habitation for fear of themselves being poached.

With humankind's proximity and behaviour having such knock-on effects even on animals in reserves, it seems that unless a much greater portion of her territories are restored, and she is left in peace to live as her true nature dictates – neither of which appear, as I write in 2005, to be particularly likely – it may be that her real history, her *natural* history, will forever remain unknowable.

Archetypal view of an Indian tiger.

Henri Rousseau
('Le Douanier'),
*Tropical Forest:
Battling Tiger and
Buffalo*, 1908,
oil on canvas.

There are, however, certain elements of her behaviour that seem to remain relatively constant and one of these is her supreme ability as an ambush predator. The complex pattern of irregular body stripes, horizontal leg patterns and intricate face markings which seem so vivid to us when we see her in captivity, contrive to make her virtually invisible in habitats as different as lush jungle, dusty, deciduous forest and elephant grass. This magical fur cloak gives the tiger many advantages. She may sleep peacefully in sunlight and moonlight without her prey species disturbing her with their alarm calls, she is concealed from her prey until the exact moment she chooses to pounce and, if she can resist fleeing when beaters try to flush her out, poachers will fail to spot her.

The tiger does not pursue her prey. Instead, tail swishing, she wanders casually through her territory, sometimes visiting familiar haunts where she expects to see her favourite meals – sambar (the largest Asiatic deer, weighing 270 kg and standing 1.5 m at the shoulder) and chital (a white-spotted deer), as well as more difficult dinners, including wild boar, crocodile and the great water buffalo. She meanders seemingly at random until she locates a suitable victim. Her initial tactic is to circle around the animal at a distance to locate a direct path through any cover. Thick-cushioned paw pads naturally muffle the tiger's tread, but to ensure an absolutely silent approach she places her hind paws directly in the pug marks of her front ones. Adopting a crouching position she moves stealthily forward, all the while making lightning calculations of the speed, height and direction of the spring needed to land on the back of her prey, near its neck. Having confirmed her prey's precise position, she slowly raises

A skull and other tiger bones recovered at India's Pench National Park in 1998.

A tiger skeleton, from the Comte de Buffon's *Histoire naturelle* (1759–67).

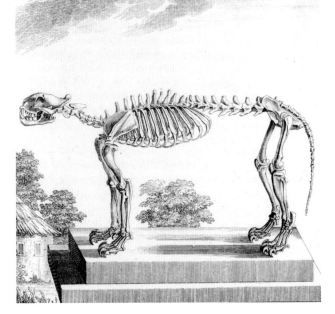

her body, and tail erect, magnificent claws unsheathed from heavy, velvet pads, charges, leaps into the air, and landing on her prey's back, makes a single, often decisive, bite on the neck, places one paw on the animal's face and another on its shoulder and uses all of her massive strength to force it to the ground. The main neck joints are crushed and compression of the spinal cord kills in a mere 35 to 90 seconds. Should her prey be larger than her, or an unusual shape, for instance a monkey, she often chooses to kill by suffocation and goes for the throat. It would seem there is never hope for the prey, but even if the tiger's aim is 100 per cent accurate, which sometimes it is not, if the creature rushes forward so it is under the tiger at her spring's highest point – a good two feet higher than where she intends to land –

the tiger, unable to change her trajectory, will fail to make contact and generally abandons her attack, not deigning to waste her remaining energy by giving chase. If she fails to kill her prey outright she does her best to secure a grip on its body and bring it to the ground by sheer force, or alternatively to hamstring it or break its leg, so she can kill it with ease when on the ground.

But even this finely tuned predator fails to kill more than around 10 per cent of the time. If her initial spring is ill judged, she has no second chance, as every creature in the area is now aware of her presence. And prey often fight back. Large antelope and deer can throw her off their backs or wrench themselves free as she attempts to incapacitate them. The wild boar, an animal of unparalleled ferocity and strength, may charge the tiger and a fight to the death ensue in which the tiger is far from always the victor. Another fearsome foe is the porcupine, which, at great speed, runs backwards towards the tiger and shoots quills into her. The tiger may kill the porcupine, but the quills remain imbedded in her throat or paws and the wounds often turn septic, preventing the tiger from hunting efficiently which may, in time, kill her. Tigers on the whole know to treat this small creature with respect and the porcupine may take liberties undreamt of by other animals, such as taking grain left next to a tiger's kill.[10]

The tiger only kills out of necessity, prompting Sankhala to write, poignantly:

> Animals know that unlike man, the tiger is satisfied with what he has killed for the day and is not concerned with tomorrow. He takes only what he needs and does not kill for the sake of killing. There is a perfect understanding between predator and prey. For the first time I felt

A family group of tigers keeping cool in the heat of the day in an Indian national park, 2004.

ashamed of being a man, who is not even trusted by the jackals, much less the deer and antelopes.

This characteristic means that sambar stags will drink almost next to a feeding tiger – tigers like to drink while eating and also use the water for cooling off – while their hinds and fawns sit only a hundred yards away completely unconcerned, something that is still observed today.

Sankhala fed his tiger charges at Delhi Zoo 3,500 kg of meat a year, which is probably less than they require in the wild. With a 90 per cent failure rate the tiger must work hard for her dinner, and the routine business of forest life such as patrolling territory and vying for a mate all consume calories, but it is reasonable to assume that the absolute minimum requirement would be one well-padded spotted deer a week. And even in a forest with adequate herbivores to sustain its tiger populations, such as Panna, in Madhya Pradesh, there can be further obstacles to the tiger obtaining her dinner in the form of wild dogs. These dogs move in packs through vast areas and are subject to boom and bust cycles – often caused by outbreaks of rabies. They appear at Panna on average every four years, usually staying a season from February to October. For the tigers, this is a very difficult time. The dogs, pursuit predators of great stamina, unnerve the forest herbivores, who become hyper-alert and issue alarm calls constantly, upsetting every denizen of the forest from langur monkey to peacock, both also occasional dinner for the tiger. Relying as she does on ambush, and having no stamina for pursuit, the tiger is now severely compromised, because her prey is constantly on the move. Tigers are often forced to move to other areas and their previous territory is taken by the arboreal leopard, who can dine on creatures inhabiting the canopy. When the dogs leave, the leopards proliferate further but the tigers return to reclaim their territory and kill the cubs of this rival predator, thus redressing the balance.[11]

Once the prey is taken, dressing dinner is a long and involved task. First the tiger pulls the hair off a section of the deer's haunches and then, using her tongue, which is covered with horny pointed sheaths that 'stick into one's fingers like so many pins',[12] scrapes away the skin. She then bites into the body and feeding can begin. Alternatively, like the wolf, she breaks open the abdomen, eats the contents of the stomach, and then moves on to internal organs.

Tigers are individual in their eating habits. Some eat 27 kg of flesh at a sitting and never return to their kill, others like to eat their dinner over a period of days, some like flesh that is 'high' (slightly decomposed), as it is softer and easier to eat. But whatever her fancy, the tiger can be certain that if it is left unguarded her hard-won feast will be reduced to hooves and dry bones by patient leopards, jackals or hyenas and, worse, ill-intentioned humans can pinpoint it, and thus in turn her, by the vultures and crows hovering overhead. Some hide their prey, dragging it

Jean Dunand
(1877–1942),
*The Forest, or Tiger
Quenching its
Thirst,* eggshell
lacquer.

into undergrowth and covering it with earth, dry leaves and
stones. One tiger in Billy Arjun Singh's sanctuary in the Terrai,
used to swim across a river, her prey gripped in her teeth, and
submerge the body next to the far bank, which prevented terrestrial scavengers from following the scent and provided the
tiger, who liked sitting in the water while eating, with a cool,
refreshing and convenient drink.

When times are hard, as they were during the Raj, and still
can be, even in reserves tigers will fight each other to the death
for a kill. If they are to survive, they have no alternative.
Sometimes the weaker tiger will give way because in the jungle

even a quite small wound can be fatal. Tiger's saliva, like that of the dog, and humanity's to a lesser degree, is antiseptic and constant licking can prevent infection. However, even trivial wounds on the back where the tiger's great pink tongue cannot reach can be fatal because maggots soon colonize the wound, burrow their way through the tiger's living flesh and finally attack her brain. Tigers have been seen rolling in mud to patch back wounds. The mud may itself have medicinal properties but importantly it prevents the maggots gaining ingress. Other self-medications include eating grass and mud to aid digestion and rid themselves of parasites such as worms.

In reserves tigers are generally seen dining alone, although mothers always share their kill with their cubs, and will allow the cubs to eat their fill before they themselves dine, even if they

Charles Verlat, *Buffalo Surprised by a Tiger*, 1853, oil on canvas.

are extremely hungry. But from time to time tigers, particularly those who are courting, can be seen sharing kills, and there have been examples of up to nine related tigers dining on the same carcass.

It is extremely difficult to follow the lengthy mating rituals of tigers in the wild and a rare and wonderful experience to watch even a part of the passionate tiger's complex courtship and love-making. A tigress first comes into oestrus when she is about three and thereafter about every 25 days until she becomes pregnant. She announces her imminent fertile period by repeatedly scent-marking the borders of her territory with a musky fluid mixed with urine and by roaring lustily and incessantly '*Aung oo oo aongh Aooch aooch aoonch aounch aoo*',[13] into the forest until one or more males are summoned. Males must fight tooth and claw for the right to mate. Enraged and excited they will rip one another's flesh and continue the duel until exhausted while the sleek object of their passion watches unconcerned and grooms her glistening fur, waiting for the victor. One such self-assured tigress having had three tigers vie for her favours

> became kittenish, and started playfully clawing her new found mate as he licked her on the neck. They played there happily for a while, and then suddenly she sprang up and bounded swiftly away into the jungle, and he followed, racing after her at terrific speed. I last saw them tearing along together, bounding over huge tussocks of grass.[14]

Although there are moments of tenderness, particularly in the early stages of courtship the female can be very rough with the male, slapping him hard with her paw, but he tolerates such behaviour, not wishing to upset her.

The tigers may make love for five days and at the height of their passion copulate as frequently as 50 times in a day, the female rubbing herself seductively along her mate's flank or nuzzling his neck to arouse him. But when mating the tigress is in an extremely vulnerable position, the tiger's full weight is on her back and he has the skin round her neck gripped firmly. Small wonder the moment he has climaxed she throws him off, boxes with him, even drawing blood, and then drops to the ground exhausted, only to succumb to desire again minutes later.

Particularly during the latter stages of pregnancy, the tigress is vulnerable to both attack and starvation. Less agile than normal and yet requiring more food, she is alone and must fend for herself, but at least her gestation period is a relatively short 15 weeks. When tiger slaughter has been particularly savage, tigresses will give birth to as many as seven cubs, evolution's method of redressing the balance, but when the tiger population is fairly stable, the usual number is two or three.

The cubs weigh about 1.1 kg and are 22–39 cm long. Like the offspring of most predators, they are born blind, which prevents them leaving the den, 'which is usually a dense patch of cover or a rough shelter of rocks',[15] and getting into danger while their mother is out hunting. Extremely protective of her cubs, the tigress will grasp them by the scruff of their necks and move them to another secret location on the slightest pretext. Like all mammals, the cubs' first food is their mother's milk which they stimulate by pressing around her nipples with their strong little paws and early on they create a teat order, which establishes who will be top cub later in life.

The cubs' wide, inquisitive amber eyes are open by the time they are two weeks old, two weeks later their vital canines are fully formed, and at two months they are enjoying their first flesh. As they develop physically they become bolder, leaving the safety of the den to rush at crows and frolic, but the moment their mother senses danger she makes a curious, almost bird-like, sound and her cubs immediately take cover. Mother and cubs have a passionate relationship, nuzzling and cuddling together and purring ecstatically for the sheer joy of being together. Tigers greet one another by rubbing their face glands together just as domestic cats do, and when a tigress has been separated from her cubs they also indulge in this ritual, creating an inclusive scent, a group identity. At around eight months, playtime is over, the serious business of learning to hunt must begin and they become their mother's constant companions. She shows them where the water holes are, where the sambar gather, the wild boar root and the langur monkeys swing through the trees. She teaches them to stalk peacock and hares and to beware the fearsome tusks of the boars. But this is cub-play; if the youngsters are to survive they must be able to bring down much larger prey. As training, their mother will disable a deer, either by hamstringing it or perhaps biting right into the muscles of its rump, then allow her cubs to kill it. They soon learn.

Hunters writing during the Raj insisted that the cubs' father played no part in their upbringing but it seems this was either erroneously reported or behaviour which had mutated due to intense persecution. Hanley observed many tiger families in the undisturbed forests of deep Assam and observed that although the father seemed to be absent while the cubs were very small, he returned when they were around four months old and took an active part in their schooling. Males, just like domestic tom-cats, often had two or three families of various ages that they visited constantly, tracking their whereabouts by following the tigress's scent spraying. The females had tight, discrete territories while the males' territories overlapped one another and might cover the territory of up to four tigresses. Contemporarily, tiger families in Ranthambore have been seen relaxing together in its pools and the parents seen co-operating on a kill and then sharing the feast with their cubs.

The male's presence is also essential for the survival of the cubs. By constantly patrolling his territory he keeps other rampant males at bay, who, keen to further their own bloodline, will kill cubs that are not their own and then mate with their mother. Naturally sometimes the incumbent male is defeated and a new genetic line established. This in itself is important for diversity as a dominant male will continue to mate with his original consort or her adult female offspring. Sometimes the incumbent's consort is pregnant when he is defeated and in this case to save her cubs the tigress will, even though she is not in oestrus, cunningly mate with the male to fool him into thinking the cubs are his own.

Cubs that survive to two years of age have learnt all they can and must leave home to wander their forest heritage, forge their own kingdoms or find a worthy mate. Their mother will come into oestrus, and roar into the velvet dark night to attract the strongest and most virile males to her side.

The cycle of life has begun again.

2 Earthly Passions and Spiritual Balances

If the lion because of its crowning mane and sandy gold pelage has been symbolically associated with regal beneficence and solar fire, the tiger, sleek and exotic, its rippling muscle hidden beneath lustrous velvet fur, embodies things far more fundamental and primordial: the essences of male and female sexuality and their attendant energies; lithe sensuality; potency, fecundity and procreation. The tiger, unlike the lion, gregariously congregating in savannah and plain, its life an open book, is a creature of mystery, of darkness and magic. Her gorgeous coat, so striking and vivid when seen in a zoo or other place of human imprisonment, renders her virtually invisible in the dappled green forests, snowy wastes and Nepalese Terrai that are her home. Now you see her, now you don't. The tiger melts so seamlessly and silently into her world that she might be a phantom, a wraith from a dimension we can only imagine in our dreams. Unlike the other big cats she not only inhabits earth, but the feminine, intuitive and creative medium of water. She luxuriates in the cool dark waters of hidden jungle pools, swims powerfully along the impenetrable waterways of the Sundarban's mangrove swamps, and glides through the ocean's foaming waves.

She announces her fertility by repeatedly scent-marking the borders of her territory with a pungent, thick, musky fluid and

Tigers mating in
Ranthambore
Tiger Reserve,
Rajasthan.

In order to mark
his territory by
spraying, the tiger
must reverse his
penis through his
hind legs.

roaring lustily until one or more males respond. The embodiment of liberated lascivious female desire, she allows them to fight without quarter for the privilege of enjoying moonlit nights and torrid days of violent unremitting passion, in which the victor may mount her as many as 50 times. Even today, Rajasthani men boasting of their masculine potency refer to themselves as 'two-legged tigers'.[1] The quintessential sexual energies of the tiger have, over thousands of years, become indelibly stamped on the psyche of the peoples who found themselves sharing her wild elusive empire. And nowhere is this more evident than in China.

Once the flesh and blood tiger roamed regally through China's dark pine forests, lazed in mountain lakes in the heat of summer, padded on the edge of desert sands. Although she is now extinct in this territory, in part because of her extraordinary symbolic power, her soul remains visible in the harmonious and aesthetic pattern of China's very landscape, in the location of its thriving, vibrant cities and in Taoism, whose all-

A tiger clearly showing the Chinese character for 'king' on its brow, as all tigers do.

pervasive energy regulates the harmony of all opposites. Her celestial self, in the form of the White Tiger, is ruler of the winds and the dark, fertile, feminine power of yin whose energy pulsates through the undulations of the earth. And yet she provides protection to esteemed ancestors, guards temples, and the Chinese character for 'king' is clearly stamped in the glistening gold, black and white markings of her brow, proclaiming her the puissant masculine ruler of the forest and potent symbol of the emperor, the nation and its military might. She is a protective and devoted mother who will pursue those who poach her cubs with the utmost ferocity; she is languid during the coruscating heat of the day yet the earth's supreme predator. She is masculine energy in feminine form and feminine energy in masculine form: the alchemy and synthesis of creation.

Contemporary Chinese calligraphy for 'king'.

Thousands of years ago the Chinese divided the celestial sphere into four quarters. The south was ruled by Vermilion Bird, the north by Black Tortoise, the west by White Tiger and the east by her counterpart, embodiment of masculine yang, lord of the oceans, spirit of water and rain, mighty Azure Dragon. Vermilion Bird and Black Tortoise rule summer and winter and are thus the great and ultimate forces of yang, sun and heat and yin, moon and cold. But in accordance with Taoist principles, Azure Dragon who presides over spring and thus the ascendancy of yang culminating in summer retains within itself elements of yin, while White Tiger presiding over autumn and the ascendancy of yin culminating in winter contains within itself the seeds of yang. Just as the sexual nature of humans carries within itself elements of the opposite sex, so White Tiger and Azure Dragon balance one another with their contrasting qualities and activities. Their dualism is represented in the heavens by the constellations of Scorpio (Azure Dragon) and Orion (Orion's head representing that of White Tiger) 'who chase one another

Que retro ſr̃ obliuiſcens ad deſtinatũ ⁊ ꝯclo biñ
uiñ ſupñe uocacionis. Et dñs in ciñgtio diɫ. Si
intte mortuo ſepelire mortuo. Tu aũ uad.s ẽstre me

igris uocata ꝓpr̃ uolucr̃ fugã. Ita. ɧ. uo
minãt ꝑſe greci ⁊ medi ſagitta. Eſt enim
beſtia uarijs diſtincta macłis. uirtute ⁊ ueloci
tate mirabilis er cui noïe flum tigs appellaꝞ
ꝗ̊ bic rapidiſſim̃ ſit oïuum fluuioꝞ. bas mag
burcania gignit. Tigs ũ ũ uacuũ raptẽ ſobo

eternally across the heavens, and so are marked out as an opposing pair'.[2] As above, so below, and the spirits of White Tiger and Azure Dragon find their counterparts on earth, imbuing it with their energy, settling in hills, mountains, valleys or other configurations which to the human mind resemble their form.

From this belief developed the venerable art of geomancy or *feng shui*, in literal translation 'wind' (White Tiger) and 'water' (Azure Dragon), which underpins the entire pattern of the Chinese landscape both natural and man-made. *Feng shui* dictates where ancestors may be fortuitously buried, great cities founded, office skyscrapers erected and even the most humble of dwellings situated. For any location to be favourable, the energy or *chi* which pulsates through everything on the earth, both animate and inanimate, needs to be harmonious and strong: the White Tiger and the Azure Dragon must, as the ancient geomancers described it, 'lie in a bow shaped line in mutual embrace'.[3] The most propitious placing of the dragon and the tiger is when together they form a horseshoe: that is to say when two chains of mountains, hills or graceful undulations curve in to the left and right and meet in a horseshoe shape. The most propitious combination is for the eastern dragon to comprise high hills, ridges or mountains and for the energy of the western tiger to be in lower undulating curves, the *chi* being at its most powerful where the sexual energies of the tiger and the dragon conjoin.

The dire consequences of ignoring the power of these energies is demonstrated by the inauspicious siting of the grave of one of the ancestors of the then ruling Han dynasty, commented on in AD 219 by Kwan Loh, considered the greatest geomancer and astrologer of his time.

Folklore tells of how poachers fleeing with tiger cubs, may distract its mother by throwing her a mirror. Miniature in an English bestiary, *c.* 1200.

An engraving of 'the rock which is called dragon and the tiger' on a mountain in Kiamsi province, China; from Athanasius Kircher, *China Illustrata* (1667).

The Black Warrior [the tortoise] conceals his head, the Azure Dragon has no feet, the White Tiger holds the corpse in its jaws and Vermilion Bird is wailing piteously; the grave being placed under the protection of four imminent dangers it must surely entail the extermination of the clan and this will happen within two years.[4]

And so it came to pass – the Han dynasty collapsed.

The siting of Guangzhou (Canton), a bustling and prosperous city since its inception, could not be more different. To the east lies a chain of hills known as White Cloud, representing the dragon, while to the west, lower undulating ground is the perfect embodiment of the tiger. The ground where they meet is the most auspicious of all and here the best side should be hidden 'like a modest virgin, loving retirement', for it is crucial to find a recess, where 'the dragon and tiger may mate secretly'.[5] As in the earth so in flesh – if it is important for the energies of yin and yang to meet in the geography of the land, then how much more so must it be for them to meet in humanity, in uninhibited and emotionally open sexual union. The earliest surviving text for the *Yi Ching* or 'Book of Changes' dates from the Han dynasty (206 BC to AD 220) and states that the interaction of one yin (woman) and one yang (man) is called Tao (the supreme path or order), the resulting constant generative process is called 'change' and that sex between man and woman gives life to all things.

The perfection of this union is symbolized in the perfect balanced symmetry of hexagram number 63 where the top trigram K'an represents yin, west and White Tiger while the lower trigram Li represents yang, east and the energies of the Azure Dragon.

In sexual metaphor, the yang dragon represents not water but fire because it rises with speed and is easily extinguished by the yin tiger or female sexuality. Unsurprisingly, yin tiger takes on the form of water, which literally extinguishes fire and, as with feminine sexuality, takes a long time to heat up but cools slowly. Sex was often referred to as 'making dragon and tiger sport', and Azure Dragon and White Tiger are constantly used in Taoist magical and alchemist literature to symbolize sex and the different potencies of man and woman.

Many Taoists sought through alchemical and sexual practices to discover the elixir of life and immortality. In alchemy White Tiger becomes yang – man, lead and fire – while Azure Dragon becomes yin – woman, cinnabar and water. In alchemy red cinnabar combines with white lead to give birth to mercury – the Great Beginning. The sexual yoga which Taoists practise is also often called the art of the White Tiger and the Azure Dragon and concentrates on the mingling of yang with yin as a means to reaching inner harmony and even immortality. Yang or dragon energy is seen as limited, and semen a man's most precious possession and something to be conserved. However, during intercourse he absorbs more and more of his partner's limitless yin or tiger energy. This adds greatly to his vitality and if just before orgasm he restrains himself then his intensified yang will flow up his spinal column, fortifying his brain and body. His partner benefits too because her yin is also stirred, reaching its apex during orgasm. Indeed for both parties to benefit in vitality and health it is essential that the woman is utterly satisfied on every occasion. The important ancient Mawangdui Taoist manuscript discovered in China's Hunan province in 1973–4 recommends many styles of harmonizing and health-giving sex, the first being tiger style, in which 'the woman crouches on hands and knees like a tiger, with arched back, while the man crouches on his knees behind her embracing her around the waist and penetrating her from behind'.[6]

A Taoist mystical sect known as the Yellow Turbans who rebelled against the Han dynasty in AD 184 were great proponents of random and open sex and believed that it absolved all sin and disabled calamity, sentiments which made the Buddhists their committed opponents. Their manual, the Yellow Book, advocated that their members 'Make Dragon and Tiger sport together according to the rules for the 3–5–7–9 strokes, the heavenly and earthly net. Open the Red gate, insert the Jade stalk. Yang will imagine the Mother of Yin white like jade, Yin will imagine the father of Yang fondling and encouraging her with his hands.'[7] This interchange of yin and yang, of

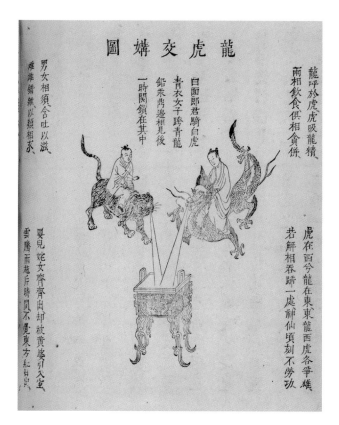

龍虎交媾圖

龍呼放虎虎吸龍精
兩相飲食俱相貪

白面郎君騎白虎
青衣女子跨青龍
鉛汞兩邊相見後
一時閞鎖在其中

雄雄錯綜以類相求
男女相須含吐以滋

嬰兒姹女齊齊出却被黃婆引入室
雲騰兩花斤時閞不覺東方紅日出

虎在西分龍在東東龍西虎各爭雄
君解相吞歸一處神仙頃刻不勞功

A Chinese alchemical illustration of the marriage of the tiger and dragon, through which Taoists sought to discover the elixir of life and immortality, *c.* 1615.

tiger and dragon, is also seen in ritual bronzes, starting at the time of the Western Zhou dynasty, when dragons became more like tigers and tigers took on dragon qualities, producing a sensuous and sinuous hybrid. A tiger, for instance, might take on the stance of a dragon, its head reversed looking towards its tail.[8] The Eastern Zhou dynasty (770–481 BC) was particularly rich in tiger-like dragons, which in reference to the fertile confluence of these energies are usually called *chi* dragons.

The tiger also plays an important part in Chinese astrology, which revolves around the lunar calendar, introduced by Emperor Huangdi in 2637 BC. This ancient system has a 60-year cycle composed of five simple cycles, each 12 years in length, which corresponds to the solar day, which is split into 12 two-hour blocks. Legend has it that when Buddha summoned the creatures of the earth to bid him farewell, only 12 attended. To commemorate their devotion, he named a lunar year after each of them, in the order in which they had arrived. Third was the tiger, which means she rules the mysterious hours of 3 to 5 a.m., when the moon bathes the earth with the power of yin. On the world stage the year of the tiger ushers in dramatic and extreme events: politics sizzle, scandals abound and fortunes are lost and made. On a personal level Chinese astrologers believe that the creature ruling both the year and time of your birth 'hides in your heart', influencing your personality and destiny. Perhaps, then, it comes as no surprise that America's ultimate sex symbol, Marilyn Monroe, was born in the year of the passionate darkly feminine tiger, as was Ho Chi Minh, founder and president of the Democratic Republic of Vietnam, the first military leader to defeat America, who partakes of the tiger's masculine association with military might.

Hong Kong Chinese stamps to mark the Year of the Tiger, 1998. The next Year of the Tiger falls in 2010.

Unfortunately for the tiger, its association with sexuality and potency in Asia has meant that for hundreds, if not thousands, of years, its penis, kidney fat and other body parts have been considered an aphrodisiac. An early reference appears in a sixteenth-century Chinese Materia Medica.[9] Of course, the tiger's penis is no more an aphrodisiac than the beautifully phallic spears of fresh green asparagus that rise from the earth in spring – but myths that are woven into cultural heritage take a very long time to die. In the twenty-first century, where millions upon millions of individuals are extraordinarily wealthy, price is no object in obtaining this legendary flesh. Rewards are large for those who deal in tiger body parts, and for the poachers themselves, even though they receive only a fraction of the end price, it is still a worthwhile financial enterprise. However, demand by factories in Thailand that manufacture patent 'medicines' containing tiger bone for the traditional Chinese medicine market to 'treat' rheumatism and from other end users interested in its 'power' to sustain erections – 'tiger penis is soaked with an exotic liqueur which is quaffed at high end Chinese brothels[10] – has been so great that it has already given the death knell to Chinese populations, reduced the Thai population to well under 150 and is now heralding the tiger's extinction in India. Indeed, as I write in 2005, the entire tiger population of Sariska Tiger Reserve in Rajasthan has 'disappeared', as has 50 per cent of the tiger population of Panna Tiger Reserve in Madhya Pradesh.

In Thailand and China factory farms now breed tigers for their body parts, although this is strictly illegal. On 25 December 2002, the Sri Racha Tiger Zoo – a Thai commercial enterprise where tourists may ogle cubs who have been taken early from their mothers and made to suckle from sows in metal farrowing crates – exported 100 of their tigers to Sanya Love World

Factory-farmed tiger cubs suckling on a sow, Thailand, 2000.

in China. A year earlier a report conducted by the Environmental Investigation Agency into Thailand's tiger economy found several 'medicines' derived from tiger bones on sale at the zoo's own Traditional Medical Clinic.[11] Sanya Love World is a theme park zoo in the Sanya Maitree Beach Resort, which has also bought in a large number of alligators to be displayed in the zoo. Reuters quoted a woman from Sanya Maitree who allegedly said 'We will also build restaurants to let people taste alligator meat. After we have bred tigers for a few years, tourists are likely to eat tiger meat at Sanya.' Sanya's general manager, Chi Zengqing, denied the report, saying it would be impossible, unless UN animal-protection policies changed.

Asian commercial interests lobby CITES keenly for the legality of tiger farms, saying it will reduce the pressure on wild populations. However, as it costs only the price of a bullet to kill a wild tiger while raising one to adulthood in a farm would cost a minimum of $2,000,[12] clearly the incentive to poach remains high. If trade in body parts were legal it would simply stimulate demand further, encourage poaching and further undermine rangers who risk their own lives in the field.

A more poignant fate for a top predator who epitomizes wild freedom and sexuality can hardly be imagined than to be farmed and killed for a fantasy aphrodisiac. This is doubly so when the drug Viagra can relieve even seemingly incurable cases of impotence. Curiously, Viagra, or Vyaghra as it is spelled in Sanskrit, the language from which both Hindi and Urdu are

A northern Indian temple wall-painting of Siva wearing a tiger-skin loincloth.

A Deccan school miniature of Siva and his wife Parvati on a terrace, *c.* 1800.

derived, means tiger. However, according to Pfizer, who manufacture the drug, this seemingly obvious reference to the tiger's
legendary sexual prowess is just a striking coincidence.[13]

In the Indian subcontinent the tiger also surfaces as a symbol of potency, fertility and sexuality. However its flesh, blood
and bone are not used as would-be aphrodisiacs and one of its
most frequent associations is with the conquering and transforming of earthly passions into mental and spiritual force.
Lord Siva, devastatingly handsome, erotically charged, faith-
ful husband yet irresistible lover, is the destroyer, the third
form of the Hindu trimurti after Brahma the creator and Vishnu
the preserver. His destruction is, however, positive as it both
purifies by destroying evil and creates the conditions for
creation. His symbol, worshipped alone, is the phallic linga
'swollen with all the potential of future creations'[14] and the
glorious fertility of humanity and nature, and in his personal
form he is almost always pictured wearing a tiger skin or sitting upon one.

In the first part of the twentieth century hundreds of beautifully worked copper tablets and seals were unearthed at the
4,500-year-old Indus Valley site of Mohenjo Daro. One depicts a
buffalo, a rhino, an elephant and a tiger surrounding a man who
is seemingly a proto-Siva in his guise as Pasupati, Lord of the
Animals. Although Pasupati is generally thought of as ruling
domestic animals, he may also have been seen to rule wild creatures, who to a god were surely as tame as mere cattle were to
man.[15] Siva has also long been associated with the tiger's power,
sexual passion and procreative prowess. Even disguised as a
religious mendicant, Siva's sublime beauty made him irresistible
to the consorts of the wise men who dwelt in his forest retreat.
Enraged, the sages used their magic to compel a great tiger to leap
from a hidden pit and attack this supremely masculine being.

Siva single-handedly slew the feline and from that time on wore its skin as a symbol of his power.

Some see Sambo's victory over the tigers in the classic children's tale *The Story of Little Black Sambo* as a metaphor for Siva's power, particularly as Siva Shambo is a dance in honour of this munificent god. Whether Helen Bannerman had this in mind when she wrote it for her children in 1899 does, however, seem open to debate. Sambo was walking through the jungle in new and gorgeous finery – red coat, little blue trousers, purple shoes with crimson soles and crimson linings and a green umbrella – when a succession of tigers, seeing him as a toothsome snack, announced their intention to eat him. Vain creatures that they were, Sambo was able to outwit them by giving each an article of his wondrous attire, causing each tiger to believe it was the 'grandest tiger in the jungle'. Soon the tigers were quarrelling over just who was the grandest and took off the finery to fight. Eating one another's tails they became tangled round a tree, and running faster and faster and faster they melted entirely into ghee.[16] Sambo reclaimed his clothes and in the ultimate demonstration of power took the morphed tigers home for his mummy to make pancakes with.

In time, subduing a tiger became a metaphor for the conquering of earthly passions and, as a symbol of their spiritual power, yogis meditated naked in the wilderness, seated upon tiger skins, and were credited with having the power to tame corporeal tigers. The great Mughal emperor Jahangir wrote in his memoirs that a group of yogis, one of whom was completely naked, were among an excited audience gathered to watch a fight between a bull and La'l Khan, a very tame tiger from his menagerie. The tiger was immediately attracted to the nude yogi and 'by way of sport, and not with the idea of any rage, turned towards him. It threw him on the ground and began to

A Kalighat folk drawing of c. 1830 of a man (probably an image of Syamakanta Banerjee) wrestling with a tiger.

behave to him as he would towards his own female. The next day and on several occasions the same thing took place.' Did the yogi keep submitting to La'l Khan's ravishment as a public display of his own powers, did he enjoy the adrenaline thrill this intimate contact must have brought or was he simply in another mental dimension? Whatever the answer, what is certain is that he was not injured in even the smallest degree. Whether, however, this was due to magic mental energy or because the tiger, having been brought up with people since a cub, concluded that humans were properly his opposite sex – in the way that small dogs brought up exclusively with people do, and so attempt furious copulation with our legs – and thus treated the yogi with consideration, is a moot point.

Vylas from the
9th–12th century
AD Kajuraho
temple complex,
Madhya Pradesh,
India.

From the sacred yogi to the profane wrestler who vanquished tigers as a display of his earthly prowess was but a short step. Formal wrestling in sand pits has always been an extremely popular Indian sport. Prizefighters, having undergone years of arduous training which ended with their wrestling with and subduing tigers, vied for large purses in the fabulously decorated wrestling halls of the maharajas until very recently. Many wrestlers made their living fighting tame tigers in shows and circuses, but the supreme proponent of this diversion was the yogi Syamakanta Banerjee, and it was in his extraordinary performances during the 1890s that the profane once again became sacred, for it was as an ascetic blessed with extraordinary powers that he was celebrated in Kalighat art, and as a yogi that he wrestled.[17] Not blind to the requirements of the material world, even if in his heart he felt himself to be a true yogi, in 1897 following outstanding success at Fred Cook and Co's circus he started one of his own. Soon command performances at Government House Calcutta were commonplace and at the insistence of the Maharaja of Tippera he even wrestled a wild tiger captured only days previously. In 1904 he returned to his roots, establishing a hermitage at Bhawali, and in the latter part of his life wrote copiously on Vedanta, a branch of Hindu philosophy and system of Jnana Yoga that guides individuals to enlightenment.

The medieval temples at the World Heritage Site of Kajuraho in central India are renowned for their extraordinary erotic carvings. Interpretation of these sculptures varies from pornography mirroring an amoral world to vivid representations of the creative and the joy that sex brings as a natural part of life. Certainly *mithunas*, carvings of copulating couples, were seen as auspicious and were often created on doors accompanied by animals or the mythic *vyalas*, a strange hybrid creature with the body of a tiger or lion which was known throughout the Persian and Indian worlds as a protective creature and the abstract representation of sex, of *kama*. Today, the guides at Kajuraho intone repetitively that although everything is permitted the conquering of lust is the way to spiritual enlightenment. Although describing the *vyalas* as symbolically representing lust, they firmly describe them as tigers – clearly the tiger's passionate nature is truly stamped in the psyche of this world.

Other groups, tribes and individual artists in India used paintings, dance, drawings and sculptures of the tiger as a fertility symbols. One such was Ganga Devi, an extraordinarily talented painter and drawer from the Mithila region of Bihar. Weddings and the rites which surround them in the main take place in a *kohbar-ghar*, or nuptial chamber, whose walls are covered with auspicious symbols, images and motifs which focus on the union of male and female and denote fertility and regeneration. They bestow their blessing on the couple, who, after three days of chastity, finally consummate their marriage. The images include the sun, the moon, the lotus – whose stylized rendition together with creatures from the ponds in which it grows covers the front wall in a particular symbol of female fecundity – and bamboo groves, a symbol of male sexuality. The side walls of the *kohbar-ghar* are usually decorated with mythic scenes or symbols that the artist finds particularly compelling. The side wall of a *kohbar-ghar* painted by Ganga Devi is in the Crafts Museum in New Delhi. Here, in her exquisite style, she has the sun symbol of male energy above a tiger whose pelt bears the same chequerboard pattern as the thick reed mat on which the couple first make love inside the *kohbar-ghar*, a symbol of male sexual potency and erotic potential, while next to him is a stylized cub, surely representing the fruit of the couple's union. All around the tiger is stylized lotus, representing the feminine force.

The Warlis, whose entire culture is permeated by worship of the tiger god variously known as Vaghya and Vāghadeva, demonstrate their admiration for the tiger's erotic potential and luxurious fertility in dance. In November, they hold a great fertility festival, the culmination of a month's dancing, which coincides

Ganga Devi's Mithila-style *kohbar-ghar* wall painting in the Crafts Museum, New Delhi.

Bacchus riding on a tiger in a Roman mosaic found under Leadenhall Street, London, dating from the 1st or 2nd century AD.

The pregnant heroine of this Bengali scroll is protected by two benevolent, anthropomorphized tigers, c. 1800, paint on paper.

with new plants blossoming in the fields, and which ends with the *puja* of the Tiger God. For the final dance, the men and women form separate circles, their arms linked together facing inwards, and dance round a phallic-shaped musical instrument, the trumpet-like *tarpā*. They move faster and faster, round and round to the music, while the *tarpā* players 'heave up and down with their massive trumpets, performing the act of procreation, in the centre of the dancing circle'.[18] February and March, the culmination of the ritual cycle of the Warli year, require a last act to propitiate the forces of nature and set the stage for new life. It is naturally the season of marriage, but before earthly weddings may be celebrated, the feminine umbar tree, whose leaves are soothing and bless the ground with shadow, must marry the Tiger God.

The Belgian painter Jean-Joseph Weerts (1847–1927) in his studio.

The tiger, in the west a true exotic, being extremely difficult to transport from its eastern haven, was, according to Pliny, first seen at the dedication of the Temple of Marcellus in 11 BC. Tame and languishing in a cage it was probably a gift from an Indian king to the Emperor Augustus. But even caged tigers retained something of their sleek sensuality and hedonistic aura for, by the first or second century AD, Bacchus, also known as Dionysus, god of wine and mystical ecstasy, and whose cult members were known for their orgiastic behaviour, was being pictured riding a tiger. This depiction may also be a symbol of the travels he was credited with making through India.

The British, when they overran India, also recognized the intrinsic power and sensuality of the tiger. But mixed as this realization was with an imperialistic vision of the tiger as a feline representative of India the nation, they were quick to slaughter it.

A melodramatic tiger abduction of a semi-clad European female, from G. P. Sanderson, *Thirteen Years among the Wild Beasts of India* (1882).

Seeing these wholesale deaths as an image of their dominance and masculine power they transferred the sexual charge of death to the feminine by taking the gorgeous thick and vivid tiger pelts and transforming them into lifeless coats and rugs for their sexual partners or wives. Glistening, velvet golden fur morphed into skins destined to be eaten by moths and crumble in middle-class houses across the English home counties. The tiger had become more than a symbol of fecundity and fertility but had taken on the aura of direct, particularly female, sexuality. This image seems lodged deeply in the western psyche, surfacing in art, advertising and even dreams. Salvador Dalí made concrete a dream recounted to him by Gala, his wife, in the 1944 masterpiece *Dream Caused*

A daughter of Vanity sits on a tiger-skin in a posed photo-graph of c. 1896.

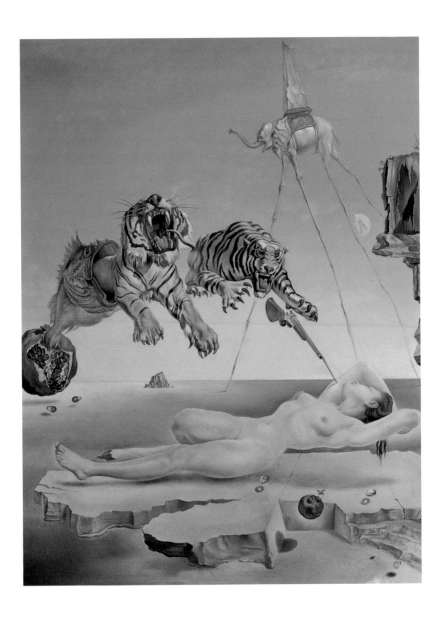

by the Flight of a Bee around a Pomegranate a Second before Awakening. Bathed in the excitement of Freud's psychoanalytical theories, Dalí announced boldly to the world that this painting was the first illustration of external stimuli influencing dream content. Here he claimed the fish represented masculine potency, the rifle with its piercing bayonet, the penis, the pomegranate feminine fecundity and fertility, and the powerful overwhelming tigers emerging from the fish nothing less than Gala's subconscious urges for sexual union given form.

Western starlets and models hoping to benefit from the tiger's reputation for sexual prowess and powerful sensuality by association posed semi-nude on tiger skins, their bright eyes with long false eyelashes shining next to the glazed glass eyes of the now dull-furred tiger, or peeped seductively out of fur coats. Not even Margaret Thatcher was immune to the tiger's powerful

Salvador Dalí, *Dream Caused by the Flight of a Bee around a Pomegranate a Second before Awakening*, 1944, oil on canvas.

Jayne Mansfield wearing leopard skin on a tiger skin.

symbolism and reflected allure: her reference to herself as a tigress garnered press in the *Sun*, *Daily Express*, *Daily Mail* and *Telegraph*. As the twentieth century marched on, the demands of status-driven western women to drape tiger pelts, along with those of the equally unfortunate leopard, over their bodies accelerated the slaughter. And even in 2004, when attitudes to this creature which hovers on the verge of extinction have reputedly changed, a window display demonstrating luxury and sensuality at Harrods, Knightsbridge, contained one such period photograph.[19]

Soon symbol had turned firmly into commodity, and with the price for skins rocketing, in the 1950s a skin cost $50, in the early 1960s $500 and by the late 1960s, in Delhi, rugs and coats were costing $10,000, killing tigers and leopards became irresistible. Poachers, so as not to damage the valuable pelts, took to wholesale poisoning, using chemicals such as DDT that polluted the entire environment. Another method which left no mark was to ram a red-hot poker into the cat's sensitive anus. Meanwhile in London, chic 1960s models posed in tiger-skin coats while clutching tiger cubs in their arms and smiling at them adoringly in unintentional irony. Prince Philip was still enjoying slaughtering tigers in Ranthambore, Rajasthan, as late as 1961.

Kailish Sankhala, tireless campaigner for the beleaguered wildlife of India, spent massive amounts of time investigating the skin trade and in 1967 the results made the front page of the *Indian Express*, causing a sensation. India was outraged and a total ban on the export of spotted and striped skins was put in place. In November 1969, the International Union for the Conservation of Nature and Natural Resources (IUCN) met in Delhi and Indira Gandhi, in her inaugural speech, declared: 'We need foreign exchange but not at the cost of the life and liberty of some of the most beautiful inhabitants of this country.'[20]

Indian servants posed among tiger-skin rugs, 1870s.

On 29 November Sankhala read his paper 'The Vanishing Indian Tiger' to the IUCN and the tiger was entered in the *Red Data Book* as an endangered species. The Report of the Expert Committee (on the decline in tiger numbers), of which Sankhala was secretary, unreservedly criticized the Forest Department for its neglect of wildlife. This enraged his colleagues but the report turned the tide of destruction and neglect and became a blueprint for future conservation measures, including the all-important Wildlife Protection Act of 1972 and the inauguration of Project Tiger, which was to pull the striped feline, at least for a time, back from the brink of extermination.

The tiger's skin and fur is no longer worn openly in the west, although it is still illegally flaunted as a trim on clothes in the east, but her sexy, potent image still speaks volumes.

In contemporary times, besides using body paint to transform themselves into an icon of feline sensuality, some individuals choose to be tattooed with her image. Entire back tattoos,

which involve severe discomfort as this is a particularly sensitive area, are very popular. Tattooing has a long history in Japan. The idea of wearing a full tattooed body suit originated around 1700 when strict laws forbade any but royalty to wear ornate clothing so instead the middle classes adorned themselves with tattoos. In Japan it developed as an aesthetic art, and during its heyday in the eighteenth and nineteenth centuries was often carried out by wood-cut artists known as *ukiyoe* who simply exchanged their carving blades for sharp needles. Their art translated beautifully onto warm flesh and the sitters literally became works of art and felt themselves imbued with the spirit of whatever person or animal, mythical or real, they adorned themselves with. Cross-cultural exchange exposed the west to these glorious designs and today clients at tattoo parlours such as Flamin' Eight in Camden, London, still favour tigers in this tradition, which is known as *horimono*. Men, in particular, see a full-back tattoo of a tiger as an expression of their virility.

The tiger also has a place in fortune-telling cards where she represents passion and the potential for new affairs, licit and otherwise, and just her name gives a product like *Tiger* beer potent sex appeal.

In a world where image is everything, the tiger's is proving to be her downfall. And, unless that image can be changed, and changed quickly, in the same way the cigarette's image as sexy accessory was manipulated by public health advertising to become that of smelly disgusting habit, the only place she will be found is in factory farms and zoos.

3 The Power of Image and the Strength of Reality

The previous chapter showed how the tiger's sexually potent and sensually alluring image has affected her personal destiny and given rise to many different forms of cultural expression. A creature as powerful and intelligent as the tiger invites humanity to manipulate her image and behaviour to enhance its own status and to further the ambitions of individuals and cultures for both good and evil. This chapter looks at some of these roles, ranging from benevolent protectress and patriotic icon to foul, fearsome and vicious killer, and also considers how her image contributed to her once very real position as guardian of the Eastern forests.

Western imperialists built up a reputation for the tiger that was almost entirely malign. Her tremendous skills as an ambush predator were taken as a sign that she was 'dishonourable', her tendency to revenge herself when wounded and persecuted to the limits of endurance as an unquenchable desire for human flesh and blood. Tribal and rural peoples were cast as being cowed, terrified and impotent against the predations of a foul feline. In one stroke the imperialists thus elevated their status above that of the natives, made comfortable slaughter from elephant back into a heroic duel, legitimized their sport and made the forests easier to destroy. These heroes left buffalo calves as bait and shot tigers from the safety of their tall

Stone tiger at an ancient Chinese tomb.

machans (hides); they shot tigers while standing upright in elephant-back howdahs, in groups of 10, 20, 30 or 40 elephants surrounded by cavalcades of beaters and others ready to despatch them should they present a problem for the so-called hunters; they shot them while they were mating and even when they were resting in their cave lairs. Hardly a hazardous occupation. It was thus vital for the machismo and status of these

servants of the Raj that the tiger was painted as a terrible, dangerous yet despicable beast.

Yet one Englishman at least, and one who knew the tiger well, Edward T. Bennett, a naturalist who for a time presided over the Tower Menagerie, defended the tiger against imperialist opinion which regarded them 'with unmingled horror' and 'detestation' and considered them ferocious with an 'insatiable thirst for blood', stating boldly that the tiger had been 'depressed and degraded beyond his natural level' and that they only consider man-eating 'when the pangs of hunger have become intolerable, and can no longer be controlled even by the over-powering sway of instinct'. Bennett also compared the tiger favourably to that feline darling of British imperialism, the lion, writing that the tiger has

> superior lightness of his frame which allows his natural agility its free and unrestricted scope, and in the graceful ease and spirited activity of his movements, to say nothing of the beauty, the regularity and vividness of his colouring . . .
> . . . he is tamed with much facility, and as completely as the lion, and soon becomes familiarized with those who feed him, whom he learns to distinguish from others, and by whom he is fond of being noticed and caressed, like the cat . . . he arches his broad and powerful back beneath the hand that caresses him.

One of his favourite charges, a Bengal tiger who was brought over on an East India Company boat, had been 'taken prisoner in company with 2 other cubs on . . . the peninsula of Malacca', where he lived

> in company with a pony and a dog, for upwards of 12 months, without evincing the least inclination to injure his companions or anyone who approached him. . . . On the voyage he was remarkably tame, allowing the sailors to play with him, and appearing to take much pleasure in their caresses. On being placed in his present den he was rather sulky for a few days but now appears to have

Return from a
tiger-hunt in
French Indochina.

recovered his good temper, and to be perfectly recon-
ciled to his situation.

Bennett put down the tiger's amiable disposition to the fact he
had never eaten raw flesh until he arrived at the Tower. This
new delight was received with great enthusiasm, but Bennett
notes that even so 'he has by no means lost his appetite for soup,
which he devours with much eagerness'.[1]

But imperialist hatred and public opinion was not to be
swayed by the opinion of a mere zookeeper. And even Rudyard
Kipling, who in *The Jungle Book* (1907) treated every animal,
including that other much maligned predator the wolf, with
compassion, wrote with nothing but contempt of tiger Shere
Khan, whom he portrayed in typical Raj-style as a man-killer

who considers the human cub Mowgli his due. Even the jungle animals despise the 'striped cattle killer' who is cast as unable to take his natural prey because of an injured paw, and further loathe him because 'man-killing means, sooner or later, the arrival of white men on elephants, with guns, and hundreds of brown men with gongs and rockets and torches'. Of course, in keeping with the culture of the time, Mowgli eventually avenges himself by leading Shere Khan into a trap where he is trampled to death by cattle. Mowgli then skins him, dances on his hide and wears his 'gay striped coat' as a symbol of his power.

Jim Corbett (1876–1955), one of the Raj's chief tiger-slaughterers, who manipulated the tiger's reputation so expertly through his bloodcurdling writing that he himself appeared as an heroic saviour, was in reality a man with a massive lust for power and status. A truly master storyteller – his swashbuckling reputedly real-life tales recounted in *The Man-Eaters of Kumaon* (1944) was even adopted as a textbook in some Indian schools – his books excited a generation of impressionable children in England and India, who longed to duel with the baneful striped predator and turn her shining, intelligent amber eyes to dust.

Man-eaters, according to Corbett, were tigers too old, too incapacitated, perhaps because porcupine quills had become embedded in their mouth or paws, a common affliction, or too ill to kill other game. Corbett's first man-eater, the Champawat, had allegedly eaten 200 individuals in Nepal before being driven out to Kumaon where in four years she had killed a further 234. After Corbett had killed the Champawat he reported that 'the upper and lower canine teeth on the right side of her mouth were broken, the upper one in half, and the lower one right down to the bone. This permanent injury to her teeth – the result of a gun shot wound – had prevented her from killing her prey, and had been the cause of her becoming a man-eater.' Even accepting this tally of human kills as realistic (and it should be noted that death by tiger was seen as a perfect cover for the settling of all too human scores), if humans were her only food, the tiger was simply not killing sufficient to survive. A tiger requires at least 68 kg of actual flesh, not flesh and bone, per week in a zoo environment to survive. Perhaps an average village woman would have weighed 50 kg (and some of the Champawat's victims were small girls); of this, her skeleton would weigh approximately 9 kg, and of the 40 kg or so left, not all would be eaten. The Champawat would be in terrible condition, half starved, and would certainly be unable, after having killed her latest victim, to have 'sprung up the side of a ravine and disappeared with her into some heavy undergrowth'.

Almost every native in Corbett's tale is in 'a state of abject terror', and in one village it was not until the great man had 'settled down to a cup of tea that a door here and there cautiously opened and the frightened inmates emerged'. Miraculously – and Corbett's tales abound with miracles – a girl who had been struck dumb when she had witnessed her sister being carried off by the Champawat regained the power of speech when Corbett told her of its death. Corbett also wrote that the fingers of the Champawat's most recent victim had been swallowed whole and categorically stated that 'it is a popular belief that man-eaters do not eat the head, hands and feet of their human victims. This is incorrect. Man-eaters if not disturbed eat everything including the blood soaked clothes.' Tiger's tongues are specifically adapted to rasp flesh from bone and unlike canine predators, who are adapted to gulp great mouthfuls down wide throats, the tiger is as fussy about its dinner as the domestic cat, and chews every mouthful carefully. Unlike canids and hyaenas, tigers do not crack open bones or gnaw on them. However, this kind of exposition makes for exciting fiction which continued during the post-Indian independence *shikar* (tiger hunting) boom, when companies arranging game-hunting trips would produce village women's bangles and declare they had been found in the stomach of the dead man-eater to excite their gullible clientele.[2]

Corbett loved hunting, and as he enjoyed the patronage of the Viceroy (Lord Linlithgow wrote the foreword to *Man-Eaters of Kumaon*), if he chose to designate a tiger as a man-eater, his judgement would not be disputed. The killing of beasts even more dangerous and malicious than the regular run of vilified tigers made Corbett appear a bigger and braver man than the other hunters, a desire deeply embedded in his psyche. Of course, he rarely put himself in real danger, unlike the Mughal emperors and the hunters of their court who relished the thrill of dangerous situations, wanting to pit themselves physically and mentally against the supreme predator. Akbar (ruled 1556–1605) often hunted with only a bow and arrow. Jahangir often hunted on foot, and although he and his entourage had guns, they often came in physical contact with the tiger and sustained very real injuries. They wrestled and rolled with only daggers and sticks to defend themselves. Naturally, the Mughals also played up the tiger's reputation but they saw her as a fearsome and worthwhile opponent even if she were 'a brute'. The courage and reputation of fearsomeness accruing to the victor was all the greater from having killed a magnificent, worthy, even regal, opponent. The tiger's reputation was such that the first emperor, Barbur, was known simply as 'the tiger' while the last, Aurangzeb (died 1707), used her as his symbol of power, adorning the hilt of his finest sword with her image. Although the Mughals kept hunting records, and like many other peoples, enjoyed animal contests, they were far more interested in accruing the kudos that came from real courage

'A Night-Watch', from G. P. Sanderson, *Thirteen Years among the Wild Beasts of India* (1882).

than tallies. The emperor Jahangir killed only 86 tigers and lions in 48 years of hunting. Bottom-of-the-rung servants of the Raj would shoot nine in a day, in perfect safety, for fun.

If western imperialism vilified the tiger in order to enhance the reputation of their agents when they slaughtered her, eastern religions portrayed her as peerless, awesome and wondrous, to elevate the reputation of their agents – monks, holy men or mythical beings – when they too killed or subdued her. The eight ancient Taoist immortals, for instance, inhabited a magical world teeming with demons, goblins, gods, dragons and, of course, tigers, and were frequently depicted as taking on the guise of a tiger to subdue or trick opponents, or subduing magnificent tigers and protecting the weak from their extraordinary depredations in a sparkling show of their fantastic and unearthly powers. As Taoism began to lose ground to Buddhism, brought to China from India by migrating Buddhist monks from around AD 200, these remarkable beings mixed with Buddhist

Wenshang Ming, one of the eight Taoist 'Immortals'.

characters in curious cultural amalgams and mythological tales which often included the fabulous striped feline.

Wu Sung fighting the tiger on Jinyang Ridge, an illustration for the 12th-century Chinese novel *The Water Margin*.

One of the most famous of these is Tripitaka, a seventh-century Buddhist, also known as Hsuan-tsang, whose real journey from China to India to find important Buddhist scriptures was made into a fabulous story by Wu Cheng'en in the middle of the sixteenth century. Tripitaka undergoes many tribulations and is on one occasion rescued from a tiger by a hunter who wrestles with the fearsome beast for an hour before finally dispatching it with 'a thrust right through the chest' and dragging it away by the ear. Tripitaka, lost in admiration, saluted him as 'a veritable god of the mountains'. The hunter's aged mother cooked the tiger flesh and laid the sizzling dishes in front of the monk. Being vegetarian he was unable to partake, but the hunter ate enthusiastically, no doubt taking on the tiger's extraordinary strength, as people hope today when they devour the flesh of factory-farmed tigers.

Monkey, a Taoist Immortal who is coerced into becoming Tripitaka's disciple, demonstrates his utter superiority to the hunter by subjugating another tiger with the five words, 'Cursed tiger stand your ground.' The tiger crouched in the dust and dared not budge. Down came the cudgel on its head. The earth was spattered with its blood. Monkey then 'undressed' the tiger. He took a hair from his tail, blew on it with magic breath, and it became a sharp little knife, with which he slit the tiger's skin straight down and ripped it off in one piece. Then he cut off the paws and head and trimmed the skin into one big square, which he wore as a potent symbol of his power.

Mere mortals were also shown to better the tiger when Chinese fiction and illustrated books began to blossom. Set around AD 1119–25 and probably conceived then, although the first extant edition is dated to the sixteenth century, *The Water Margin*, one of the most important pieces of Chinese fiction, is a long and rambling tale of bandits who roam the countryside. It is presented as illustrations with text running over it, a kind of early comic strip. The bandits represented a force of rebellion against the ruling classes of the time, against oppression, and so it is not surprising that at one point the drunken bandit Wu Sung must fight and best the predatory and fearsome tiger. Hundreds of years later children in China still thrill to this tale and Wu Sung appears in repeat after repeat on Chinese television.

In the still wild Sundarbans where, because they disturb her habitat so much, woodcutters and honey gatherers strongly feel the need to control the tiger, enhancing the ability of real and fictional holy men to control this worrisome creature is a useful socio-political tool. The native Hindu population worshipped Dakshin Roy, a local deity who was able to move the tigers where he would and thus protect his devotees. However, an immigrant Muslim population brought with them their own

goddess, the kindly Banabibi, who also controlled these felines and, over decades, even centuries, a mythology developed in which Banabibi gradually displaced Dakshin Roy through various battles and trials so that now Muslim and Hindu alike worship this essential deity.

A fight with a tiger in Chen Shaomei's 1950s illustration to a Chinese folk story.

Control of the tigers may also be seized by certain special humans, whether fictional or living, who are then elevated into gods or saints. Nowhere is this seen more clearly than in the cult of the Muslim holy man Barekhan Gazi, who also feuded with Dakshin Roy and won. The miraculous exploits of Gazi and the punishments he inflicts on those who do not worship him have been celebrated on the most beautiful Bengali scrolls. His cult was able to spread out from the Sundarbans and allowed his Muslim devotees to graphically show their Hindu colleagues their saint's power. One particularly compelling image is that of Gazi sitting on a tiger and using it as his vehicle, as did Dakshin Roy.

In the Malay peninsula the Kerinci merchants from Sumatra who used her image for their own particular ends added a supernatural twist, and claimed to be were-tigers who could change at will from their human form to that of the striped feline. First feet transmuted to enormous paws, their sheathed claws ready to tear flesh; puny human legs then grew bulky with vibrant muscle and rippled with change and colour until covered with glossy russet gold fur, a striped tail dropped between long legs and finally a massive head with strong white teeth appeared.[3] In this monumental form the were-tiger revenged himself for slights suffered in his human form, was able to eliminate unwanted mothers-in-law or unfaithful spouses and, worse still, to satisfy his tiger-hunger, killing the water buffalo which were crucial for a whole village's survival. So successful were the traders in creating this mythology that it came to be believed as an absolute article of faith throughout the peninsula. Even the Portuguese ecclesiastics in Malacca were taken in, and gravely excommunicated a number of these supernatural creatures in their human form in 1560.[4]

This malign depiction of the tiger was of course a handy smokescreen for any individuals who wanted to rid themselves of rivals or ugly wives, as it was for denizens of the Indian subcontinent, but it also allowed the traders complete licence. Although some of these traders were prosperous (gold and gold dust was panned in their area), the majority were itinerant cloth merchants or desperate beggars who by threatening a credulous population with the spectre of their were-tiger were able to have what were probably often extremely unreasonable demands complied with. At the turn of the nineteenth century this fostered reputation proved fatal for one Kerenci pedlar known as Haji, who for many years had been visiting the isolated village of Bentong. A local tiger was, at this time, taking so many of these people's water buffalo that deserting their homes seemed to be the only option. Haji was walking to the village one evening when he heard the terrible roar of the tiger. Terrified, he ran blindly until, spying a huge wooden tiger trap, he ran inside. The trap closed behind him. The tiger might roar

A scene from the legend of the Bengali saint Gazi Pir (fl. c. 1795–c. 1804), scroll painting, Bengal, c. 1800.

but Haji was safe. Morning came, and Haji waited for those he thought were his friends to set him free. The villagers, however, concluded that if he was in the tiger-trap there was only one explanation, he was the were-tiger responsible for killing the buffalo, and he was impaled on a spear in his sanctuary.[5] Whether the villagers genuinely believed this or were taking revenge for demands Haji may have made, remains unknowable.

In China, Chairman Mao branded the tiger a pest and encouraged farmers to kill them, which besides sounding their death knell, in a radical value shift effectively degraded one of China's most ancient and revered spiritual images, White Tiger, the embodiment of yin, and separated the Chinese from their heritage for political ends.

However, other tiger realities exist and reveal far more complex and fascinating pictures of their role in human culture than these malign stereotypical manufactured conceits. Power, after all, can be used to help and protect, as well as to harm. The tiger once reigned supreme over her exotic, far-flung eastern empire and played an important role in the lives of the myriad people who were dependent upon the forest for their livelihood, such as honey collectors and those who made beautiful jewellery from the lacquer of the chila tree as well as those who simply lived on its bounty.

The tiger, although on the one hand a creature capable of depredation and thus to be treated with respect, on the other was their supreme ally who protected their only asset, the forest and the creatures who dwelt within it, from those who would ravish it. Who would dare to stalk the forest on a velvet moonless night and steal its wood while its incomparable lord and guardian patrolled its margins? The tiger's importance was recognized by Lord Krishna, the divine blue-skinned cowherd, one of the most popular gods of the Hindu pantheon, who describes the mountains as spirits who change into lions and tigers to protect the forest.[6] The intense feelings of these peoples is expressed poignantly in a painting which hangs in the Hwa Jang Sa temple in Seoul, entitled 'a wicked woodcutter being eaten by a tiger in hell'.[7] For people who were more gatherers than hunters, the tiger also offered sustenance. Often tiger kills are massive. The nilgai, a 'great, ungainly animal',[8] is far too big for a lone tiger to consume at one sitting, and as tigers often do not return to their kills, not only other animals but forest dwellers too gain a supply of nutritious meat which would otherwise be difficult to come by. For subsistence arable farmers the tiger was a beneficial force that despatched crop-devouring herbivores.

But the tiger was no match for the modern guns of rapacious hunters and was unable to protect herself or her people's lands against the onslaught of imperialism. She was slaughtered and huge tracts of forest were felled and plundered. A very real resentment was felt towards the killers of the striped feline whom many referred to as their best friend, and who often refused to lead white hunters to her lair, a reluctance that the hunters in ignorance attributed to fear.[9] This apology, by the chief of a team of Vietnamese Mnoogs employed to cut down a tree in the interests of western science at the end of the nineteenth century, epitomizes local people's feelings:

Spirit who last made thy home in this tree, we worship thee and come to claim thy mercy. The white mandarin our relentless master, whose commands we cannot but obey, has bidden us to cut down thy habitation, a task that fills us with sadness and which we carry out only with regret. I adjure thee to depart at once from the place and seek a new dwelling place elsewhere, and I pray thee to forget the wrong we do thee, for we are not our own masters.

The chief then, showing his respect for the tiger who as lord of the forest has jurisdiction over every tree, addressed an heart-felt apology speech to it.[10]

So very few of the forests' feline guardians now survive that many 'protected' reserves such as Bharatpur, a World Heritage site which once teemed with tigers and leopards, have none and forest destruction is immeasurable. With nothing to fear and no options, villagers now openly denude the land of wood, graze over 3,000 head of cattle there, putting the wild herbivores under tremendous pressure while pariah dogs hunt the wild deer. Although the failure of the monsoon is a factor, humanity is responsible for much of the decimation. When I visited there in 2005, this invaluable site was in the terminal stages of ruin and one resident naturalist estimated that a mere

A shot tiger on the bonnet of a Rolls-Royce Phantom at Bandh Baretha, a wildlife reserve near the city of Bharatpur, 1958.

One of the last tigers 'Shot at Bharatpur 1949'. Tigers are now extinct in this locale.

SHOT AT
BHARATPUR!
1949

10 to 30 per cent of the migrating birds who once found it such a congenial place to breed were visiting.

Many of these forest people wish to return to the time when they lived in harmony with the forests. They do not crave western education but want their children to learn the ways of the land and the skills of forest survival so that the now many desert-like areas of India may become fertile and green and the tiger again take on its ancient royal obligation to protect her people's land. A reflection of this desire, and of the burgeoning expression of artistic nationalistic opposition to the Raj's lion, is seen in many

A contemporary Indian folk painting of the demon Mahisha, who is defeated by Durga riding her tiger. Here the tiger controls Mahisha.

हरसिंह अद्

The goddess Durga on her tiger vehicle outside a temple in north central India, 1997.

depictions of the pre-eminent Hindu goddess the Devi Durga, whose vehicle in earlier times was more frequently the lion, but over the last two centuries becomes the very Indian tiger.

Feminine strength and power incarnate, a force for peace, Durga was created by the gods to keep in check the demons who were threatening the peace of the world. In a mythical version of the all too common animal contests arranged between cattle and tigers, she defeats the buffalo demon Mahisha from

The family of Chedi Mali, c. 1938, watercolour design of a tiger and a pigeon on a paper casket used for worshipping the goddess Devi. As in other examples of art in India and elsewhere, tigers are frequently shown with stylized stripes broken into long spots.

the back of her tiger. Passionate, independent and as sexually charged as her vehicle, Durga is, however, most importantly guardian of the tiger's forests and jungles, a potent symbol of mother earth, and protector of villages able to intercede with the mighty feline on her devotees' behalf. Her image stretches the length and breadth of India but her power like that of so many gods and the tiger itself now seems diminished in the face of global consumerism.

In the southern states of Tamil Nadu, Andra Pradesh and Kerala, the tiger is enthusiastically celebrated in dance at festivals to honour local deities who, like Durga, ride this feline and share much of her symbolic meaning. The dancers are usually painted in black and yellow and often wear a papier-mâché head, adorned with wool to represent the tiger's fur. In Mangalorean tradition, to express the carnivore's power a skilful dancer must perform 'many heroic acts', one of which is 'killing' a sheep, which in contemporary times means the dancer holds the sheep by his teeth, tosses it in the air and throws it away, although the sheep is not actually killed.[11] In contrast, one Captain Samuels, reporting at the turn of the nineteenth century, tells of the marriage ritual of the Gond tribe where two men, possessed by their tiger god, 'fall ravenously on a bleating kid and gnaw it with their teeth till it expires'. A sight, the Captain noted, 'only to be equalled on a feeding day in the Zoological Gardens'.[12]

In 1989 the Bengali poet, novelist and film director Buddhadev Dasgupta brought a lyrical and dream-like quality to the Tiger Dance in his highly accomplished film *Bagh Bahadur*, which juxtaposed the power of a fleshly feline with that of a Tiger Dancer who is aligned with the tiger's powers. The dancer's celebrated position is eclipsed when a circus featuring a live leopard act joins his village festival and to prove himself he must challenge the leopard to a duel.

The tiger's controlled movements, which deliver both her supreme hunting prowess and magical stalking, are another aspect that man has sought to make his own. Initially, the movements were incorporated into Hua Tuo's medical shadow boxing, a third-century forerunner of tai chi and kung fu, which the Chinese physician based on the movements of the five creatures he saw constantly around him: the deer, the monkey, the bear, the crane and the tiger. The movements were developed in the Buddhist monasteries of Shaolin by two Indian monks: Batuo, who developed jingang chan kung fu, and Bodiharma, who around AD 527 devised another sect of kung fu which endowed the monks in his care with sufficient physical strength to endure their lengthy and arduous meditations. Tiger form, representing bone development and strength, remains an integral part of these arts even today.

The tiger has also been an important symbolic and spiritual reality for those who lived and continue to live in shamanistic societies. Magnificent, supremely intelligent, and incredibly physically powerful, their association with water conferring on them the mystical ability to travel between worlds, it is surely no wonder that prehistoric hunter-gatherer cultures saw the tiger as a potent representative of natural and supernatural worlds and sought to identify themselves with the magic of the tiger and make it their own. One of the earliest examples of this exists to this day in eastern Russia.

Millions of years ago, dark thick lava flowed in a potent stream from the heart of the earth into the waters of the immense river Amur, causing the lava to crack and form enormous basalt boulders, which, in contemporary times at least, only rise from the waters at low tide. Five and a half thousand years ago the tribes living near the Amur used these monumental rocks as the canvas on which they incised striking relief drawings with flints. These petroglyphs are powerful artistic images giving us a glimpse of the creatures, mystical, magical and terrestrial, which inhabited the Amurs' world. In prime position were Black Dragon, legendary master of the river, and Tiger, lord of the forests. The form of the tiger's striped body with its round muzzle stretched can constantly be found in the nineteenth- and twentieth-century ritual shaman sculptures of the Amur nations, no doubt a tribute to the forest lord's power to assist the shaman, as is the tiger's presence on the shamans' ritual clothing.

The first ever images of the tiger: a petroglyph on basalt rock in the Amur river, southern Siberia.

As late as the 1920s the Goldis, one of the peoples of the Amur, were actively practising shamanism. Their powerful helpers were the bear, the panther and the tiger, and their initiator took the form of a winged tiger who could take the shaman to the four corners of the earth.[13] There are many anthropomorphous masks also incised on the rocks but one seems so 'beast-like, awesome and powerful'[14] that it must surely be a tiger, the emotions expressed in this exquisite art being those that these early denizens of the Amur must have felt when confronted with this mighty being. Many others seem to be part tiger, part man in aspect, surely an early representation of the shaman's belief that by taking on the aspect of an animal he may partake of its powers. In a world where man was at the mercy of the capricious spirits of animal, wind, rain and pestilence who dwelt in what contemporary western practitioners of shamanism describe as non-ordinary reality, he sought to align himself with the truly powerful and the animals who by sacrificing their bodies to him, such as elk, saved him from starvation. The tribes of the Amur, then, lived in tune with nature and accepted the tiger – *amba* – as a vital constituent of their world, a creature who like all other beasts was possessed of human characteristics and as such was kin. Venerated, this subtle feline was forgiven the occasional depredation of food or people. And some, like the Goldis, who regarded her as a sacred ancestor, ruthlessly expelled from their tribe anyone who dared kill this heavenly relative.

The tiger's image also appeared frequently on Chinese ritual bronzes, the earliest of which date back to the beginning of the Shang dynasty (1766–1050 BC). Sometimes these representations are realistic: the tiger's body may be used as a handle on a ritual wine-mixing vessel or stand as sculptural decoration on the edge of a flat bowl. Often, however, they are highly stylized designs, for Shang artists confronted with the problem of representing a curvy and distinctly corporeal creature onto a flat surface devised a solution magical in its simplicity. They split the body into two equal halves, which are arranged in symmetrical pairs. If the tiger heads face one another they become one outward-looking head with two eyes, but they can also be seen as side views of two individual tigers. A flexible and ingenious art.

Some authorities believe all these tigers, along with the images of dragons, birds etc., are merely decorative and indeed they are beautiful in their own right. However, every culture on earth was once a hunter-gatherer society confronted with the same needs and awesome terrors as the peoples of the Amur, and virtually without exception they have ancient shamanistic mythologies that tell how once man was in a state of grace, able to talk with the animals and communicate freely with the spirits of all entities, ancestors and with the gods who lived in nonordinary reality – the upper and lower worlds of this cosmology. But man always falls from this blissful state – in Christian tradi-

Sleeping on rugs woven in the form of a tiger or its skin conveyed protection from evil in the dreamer. This example is Tibetan.

tions this is represented by Eve's biting on the apple of knowledge – and becomes what he is today, mortal and obliged to toil ceaselessly.[15] Early Chinese mythology is no different.[16] After this calamity, shamans, able to enter an alternative state of consciousness and enter the reality in which these spirits dwell, become the vital link between terrestrial and celestial, the living and their ancestral gods. In this non-ordinary reality they can influence the spirits, who are as capricious as the gods of the ancient Roman pantheons, and thus alter the train of events on earth. The tiger melting in and out of the forest must have seemed imbued with magical as well as material powers, the very source of primal energy and power.

No wonder then that ancient Chinese shamans and priests wished her to be their helpmeet when they travelled to non-ordinary reality to intercede on behalf of their flocks and tribes, and that tiger images on ritual vessels served a symbolic, perhaps essential, spiritual purpose. This seems even more likely when we take into account that *wu* (animal offerings) and *chi* (ritual vessels) were fundamental components of the shaman's art. Tigers often formed the handles of bronze wine mixers, which were frequently used as ritual vessels in sacred ceremonies where some authorities speculate that flesh-and-blood tigers and oxen were sacrificed in huge cauldrons.[17] These *wu* characters also appeared frequently on tripods, and in an ancient Chinese text[18] Wang-sun Man, greeting the king of Chu on behalf of King Ding, explained that this was so the Ding people would know which animals and spirits would help them cross to heaven from earth and which would harm their efforts, so that 'all enjoyed blessings of heaven'.[19]

In India there is controversy over the meaning of the beautifully worked copper tablets and seals, frequently engraved with tigers and other important animals such as rhinos and elephants, which were unearthed at ancient Indus Valley sites of Harappa and Mohenjo Daro. Some speculate they had a magic or talismanic significance designed to keep their owners safe from the predations of wild animals or robbers in a way not dissimilar to that of western travellers' St Christopher keyrings. For who could better protect the lone traveller than the lord of the forest? Other authorities however give these seals a much darker reading, seeing them as sacrificial indicators and quoting the *Kalikapurana*, which notes 'The pleasure which the goddess [Kali] receives from an oblation of the blood of the fish and the tortoise is one month's duration . . . the blood of the wild bull and guana give pleasure for one year . . . the buffalo and rhinoceros's blood for a hundred and that of the tyger an equal number'.[20]

In China, Shang and Western Zhou (1766–770 BC) bronzes frequently feature a man with his head between or near a tiger's open jaws. A simplistic reading is that the supreme predator is preparing to devour man. Another is that the tiger in her guise of spirit of the wind, symbolized by the breath rising from her great lungs and out through her jaws, is helping a human shaman move between worlds, to rise to the heavens on the winds that are so often a necessary component of the shaman's journey. This idea is echoed in the tiger cave (*Bagh Gumpha*) of Orissa, India, where the exterior entrance has been carved into the wide-open mouth of the feline. This imagery is used to allow movement between and separation of different worlds and is common in many cultures.[21] The *Mahabahrat* has many examples of gods retiring, even hibernating, in a separate space to rejuvenate, and the void within the tiger cave suggests this is a place where spiritual merit may be gained in a different world, in a different reality.

In China the tiger was also acknowledged as spirit ruler of the winds, a position of supreme importance encapsulated in the age-old Chinese saying 'If wind and rain do not come in due proportion, there will be famine.' The fear of starvation was stamped in the ancients' psyche. Small wonder, then, that the tiger together with her elemental partner the dragon was called upon to aid puny humankind and keep balance. One way of doing this was by performing dances with intensely controlled rhythms whose beat was established by the Tiger Box or Yü – a hollowed block of wood resembling a tiger with a serrated back, which when brushed or struck with a stick gave a deep rasping noise.

The White Tiger of the West who ruled one quadrant of the heavens was also looked on as a protector against demons, ghosts and evil spirits, who would be terrified by so mighty a spirit. As early as 1200–1100 BC Chinese graves were being dug in a cruciform shape,[22] with the west to the body's left and the east to its right,[23] and by 500 BC grave sites were being altered to conform with *feng shui* principles. During the Han dynasty (206 BC–AD 25) coffins had dragons painted on their left, tigers on their right and a golden sun and silver moon on their lid to mirror the auspicious power of the celestial heavens, while small tiger carvings, often in jade, were placed to the left of the coffin to amplify its already awesome power. Sundials and cosmic mirrors inscribed with these powerful symbols were also popularly placed in graves, to accumulate and transmit vitalizing influences and so give comfort and strength to the spirit of the body within.[24] Tigers are also painted on the walls of houses and temples, they adorn the prows of ships and even today, in gaily coloured embroidery, adorn tiny children's shoes and hats. To western eyes these tigers, with their great bulging eyes and curvy, if toothsome smiles, seem genial benevolent figures, but to eastern eyes these characteristics are frightening and foreboding.

The tiger is seen as a protective and benevolent spirit in Korea, where it plays a dominant role in their creation myth, features in ancient shamanistic petroglyphs such as those at Daegokri Ulsan,[25] and is deeply woven into many facets of life and culture. Although regarded with awe, the tiger is believed to possess great nobility of spirit and be able to banish evil spirits and guard the fortunes of her people. In short, a virtual deity whose image adorns wondrous screens, garden walls and doors in almost every household, thus ensuring its protection. It is, however, as the delightful, benevolent messenger of Korea's most popular deity, San Shin, spirit of the mountain, that she is particularly revered and even Buddhism, when it swept through Korea, had to accept that the tiger and San Shin were integral to Korea's culture. Now, almost every Buddhist temple has a shrine dedicated to them.

Migrating Buddhist monks and their disciples were often depicted accompanied by tigers and the Dunhuang (Gansu province) 'library cave' on the Silk Road in China contains some beautiful examples of this painted on silk during the Tang dynasty (AD 618–907). These tigers are not threats but guardians

A 19th-century
Chinese tiger cap.

and helpers, as in the instance of Dharmatala, depicted travers-
ing the mountainous silk route accompanied by the monk
Mahakashyapa and a striped feline. Legend has it that in an
earlier incarnation Dharmatala was guarding the images of the
Buddhist *lohans*, or saints, in the great hall of a temple when he
was set about by robbers. A tiger immediately materialized from
his knee and drove away the intruders and has been his guardian
ever since. *Lohans* are also pictured with tigers, sometimes in

San Shin the Korean mountain god with his tiger, 2nd half of the 20th century, cloth backed with paper.

extremely intimate and affectionate ways, and the tiger can be seen as a symbol of the *lohans*' strength in overcoming earthly passions and an expression of their own extraordinary powers.

Fenggan Chanshi, one of the Buddha's original disciples who obtained nirvana, is also known as the Tiger-taming *lohan*. To prevent a tiger harassing his monastery he advised that it be fed with vegetarian food. Soon the fearsome predator was transformed into Fenggan Chanshi's tame familiar, accompanying him into the halls of the monastery and causing a certain amount of discomfort to the other inhabitants. The theme of vegetarianism subduing the tiger's aggression, and of course its passions, is a common one in both eastern and western minds but, in reality, the tiger, like the domestic cat, would die if deprived of flesh.

A Yi dynasty Korean painting of a tiger and a magpie, 18th century, ink and colour on paper.

A *lohan* in the Gung Bi painting style, 18th/19th century.

The tiger was also used by the Buddha to illustrate what is considered to be the greatest of all virtues, compassion. In an early incarnation on the path to enlightenment the Buddha lived as Prince Mahasattva. Walking with his brothers through lush mountains, he noticed a tigress, great ribs sticking through matted fur, lying at the bottom of a precipice delirious with hunger and about to eat her two cubs. Without hesitation, the prince threw himself on to the rocky painful ground and waited quietly for the tigress to start devouring him, but so weak was she that she could not even summon the strength to bite him. The prince then pricked his finger with a thorn, causing his bright red blood to flow forth. Licking the life-giving liquid, the tigress gained enough strength to feast upon his flesh and the

A Buddhist monk, Pra Acham Chan, surrounded by tigers at the Wat Pha Luang Ta Bua Tiger Temple, Thailand, 2004. The monks are creating a tiger sanctuary there.

lives of her cubs were saved. Fact not fiction according to Buddhist texts; a much-revered shrine marks the spot.

Still other groups and individuals use the tiger as a symbol of their own potential and actual powers in the same way that the lion has been used for hundreds of years in heraldry to convey the quality of nobility. The tiger as an emblem or logo graphically demonstrates you possess physical and mental strength and that you are quite prepared to use these powers to their fullest extent.

Unsurprisingly then she represented the medieval southern Indian dynasty of the Cholas, whose empire stretched from Indonesia in the east to Sri Lanka in the south, and continues to be the talisman of the Sri Lankan Tamil separatists (Tamil Tigers) who identify themselves with that royal house and wish to project a fearless and ruthless image.

There is however, no one, ancient or modern, who has succeeded in making the tiger their own, and projecting her power in such an intense way as Tipu Sultan (1750–1799), ruler of Mysore, by 1782 India's most powerful state and a constant thorn in the side of the British. Tipu, which means tiger in

Canarese, was named after a Canarese holy man, and from an early age he identified himself body and soul with this quintessentially Indian symbol that frequented his dreams and his life. 'Rather live two days as a tiger, than two hundred years as a sheep' was Tipu's motto. His throne, a craftsman's masterpiece, broken into pieces by the 'indiscreet zeal of the prize agents of the British army', was extraordinary:[26] a howdah, some eight or more feet in width and some five feet in depth, standing on eight tiger legs above which, decorated with exquisite tiger finials, encrusted with rubies, emeralds and diamonds, were mesmeric tiger heads; the whole supported by a life-size tiger carved from wood and covered with a thick layer of gold, worked to give the impression of the tiger's stripes. Bubris (stylized tiger stripes) adorned the uniform of Tipu's infantry and palace guards, tigers crawled over sword hilts and crouched at the muzzles of his cannons, while his weapons and ordnance bore a calligraphic representation of a tiger's face reading 'The lion of God is conqueror'. Two very live tigers were chained in the private square in

Anna Tonelli, *Tipu Sultan Enthroned*, 1800, watercolour drawing.

front of his palace; according to a Dr Buchanan, they 'although tame, would in case of any disturbance become unruly'.

Tipu had nothing but tigerish contempt and hatred for the British bandits who were doing their best to deprive him of his lands and capital, and his use of the tiger motif was, of course, a very real assertion of his ferocious nationalism. This loathing was vividly represented in various artistic endeavours. The walls of his capital were decorated with life-size caricatures of the British, a number of which featured trembling white men being seized by tigers, but his *pièce de résistance* was 'Tippoo's Tiger', a life-size wooden organ in the form of a tiger, which makes 'the growling cough of the Bengal tiger' as it devours a Britisher who emits pathetic groans.[27]

Until relatively recently it was possible to visit the Victoria and Albert Museum and bring the tiger to life by turning a handle. A favourite with schoolchildren and still remembered fondly, Tipu's tiger is now imprisoned in a glass cage for his own good. No doubt the event that inspired Tipu to commission this ingenious work was the death of the son of his implacable enemy General Sir Hector Munro, who had defeated Tipu and his father in a particularly humiliating and bloody battle in 1781. Munro junior was carried off by a tiger after a hunting spree in the wild Bengal Sundarbans in 1792. The gruesome scene was immortalized in a Staffordshire pottery group, and so keenly caught the British imagination that almost 30 years later in 1827 'The Death of Munro', 'a *new* Melo Dramatic Sketch, in One Act, written expressly to introduce Mr W. F. Woods celebrated DOG, BRUIN, in the character of a Tiger, interspersed with combats etc.' was playing to capacity crowds at the Royal Surrey Theatre, London. The theatre poster for Monday 7 May notes that 'the ROYAL TIGER's astonishing feats of agility, having been pronounced to be unequalled and his terrific seizure of Munro

'Tippoo's Tiger',
c. 1793, wooden
mechanical organ
and automaton.

received with loud cheering – he will continue his unrivalled performance every Evening'.[28]

Even the British were forced to acknowledged Tipu's tigerish nationalism, celebrating at least one of their victories over him by striking a medal depicting on one side the 'British' lion, representing dominion over Africa, defeating the tiger of India, and on the other the battle. Tipu almost restored the tiger's power but in the end he was overcome by lionish British Imperialistic force. The tiger is now India's most potent and recognizable symbol, making it is easy to forget that it was only in 1972 that she finally replaced the largely irrelevant lion as India's national animal.

Esso (Exxon Mobile in the US), the multinational oil company, also chose to use the tiger's powerful image to express the excitingly masculine power of their petrol and it is now one of the world's most easily identifiable corporate symbols. In the early 1900s 'leaping tigers graced the emblems of Tiger Benzin gasoline pumps' in Norway. Some feared that her image was so potent that drivers would be encouraged to become reckless and by 1959 she had morphed into a loveable cartoon tiger, which became such a worldwide phenomenon that *Time* magazine called 1964 'The Year of the Tiger Along Madison Avenue'. With the slogan 'Put a Tiger in Your Tank', the tiger's influence grew and grew.[29]

In contemporary times, although the tiger is still seen as a carnivore possessing enormous strength and power, that image, at least in the West, has been eclipsed by her role as the dominant symbol of worldwide environmental conservation, a phenomenon Esso were quick to identify themselves with. As concern over the tiger's extinction grew Esso lent their support to the Save the Tiger Fund and to activists like Valmik Thapar in India, who has done so much to highlight her plight. But, of course, this is simply another manipulation of the tiger's image, for Exxon Mobile is one of the main corporate movers preventing the USA signing up to the Kyoto protocol, thus making it impossible for the rest of the world to tackle the looming disaster of global warming.

The famous Esso tiger.

4 The Psychology of Fear: the Tiger Tamed, the Tiger Degraded

The tiger, for all that she may be revered and worshipped, is still a breathtaking predator, holding the power of life and death in her razor sharp claws and great canines. She inspires awe but also fear.

In western cultures, in particular, what is feared is to be exterminated, whether that fear is logical or not. In 2005 local councils in England were considering felling mature chestnut trees lest a chestnut as it drops hurts someone. But councils are only following in the footsteps of those who for hundreds of years have demanded the death of spiders, who do nothing but good by devouring flies, and that sweetest of creatures the tiny trembling brown mouse, because they are 'frightened'. What chance the tiger? As she is, unlike the mouse, not only an animal who was actually capable of damaging man but also the flesh and blood representative of a nation, very little.

As the Romans publicly degraded and slaughtered tens of thousands of lions and leopards as a demonstration of their imperial might, and effectively wiped out big cats from the Mediterranean, so the Raj, following the same agenda, slaughtered the tiger. For the British, its persecution was Indian and Burmese subjugation personified and many maharajas wishing to be identified with the new locus of power enthusiastically joined in: the maharajah of Surguja, for instance, personally killed 1,707.

This tale of Moti, a pet tiger who had been captured when a few days old and brought by the officers of a British regiment to a 'beast garden' in Lahore, is, as its author John Lockwood Kipling, Rudyard Kipling's brother, writing in 1891, notes, a perfect 'allegory of empire as well as a true tale'.[1]

Peter Paul Rubens, *The Four Continents*, 1620, oil on canvas.

Once he escaped from his den and there was wild alarm. The Jemadar or headman of the gardens, a man of great personal courage, ran across the road to government house demanding an official order from the Sircar for the arrest of the truant. Somebody gave him a large official envelope with a big seal, and thus armed the Jemadar went in chase. Moti was found on the public

A 1904 advertisement for a tiger-killing rifle in a colonial Indian newspaper.

The Prince of Wales (the future Edward VII) killed seven tigers in a single day during a royal visit to India in 1876.

promenade or Mall, very much alone as might be expected. The keeper hurried up to him, displaying the Lord Sahib's order, and shaking it in his face, rated him in good, set terms for his black ingratitude in breaking from the care of a government that fed him regularly and used him well. Then he unwound the turban from his head, and having tied it round the beast's neck, hauled him to his den, gravely lecturing as he led. Moti went like a lamb.

TIGER HUNTING ON ELEPHANT-BACK.

(From a photograph by A. G. R. Theobald.)

'Tiger-hunting on Elephant Back', from William Hornaday's *Two Years in the Jungle* (1885). High up in his houdah, and likely surrounded by other tamed elephants, this servant of the Raj is in little danger.

Unusually, Kipling saw more than a caged trophy in Moti and wrote in his memory

his skin, now in Lahore Museum, being carelessly removed does scanty justice to the memory of a beautiful beast; the only animal of my acquaintance that really liked tobacco. The smoke of a strong cheroot blown in his face delighted him; he would sidle, blink, stretch and arch his mighty back with the ineffable satisfaction that all cats find in aromatic odours.

To shriek 'we rule India', everything from wallpaper celebrating Queen Victoria's golden jubilee to silk theatre programmes carried images of the tiger, while her pelt, in an
unknowing shamanistic tribute to the tiger's own power, was
used in ceremonial army wear. Aside from imperialist consider-
ations, those in positions of overwhelming power, spiritual and
temporal, have always chosen to assert their supremacy over

the flesh-and-blood rulers of nature, be they wolves, lions or tigers, resulting in varying degrees of oppression from well-fed but deathly boring captivity to excruciating torture relished by those who inflicted it. In this way the supreme emperors and governors of earlier times and, in more democratic times, ordinary people such as circus owners, made it clear to all that they

A British soldier's tattoos of *c.* 1899, among which tigers feature.

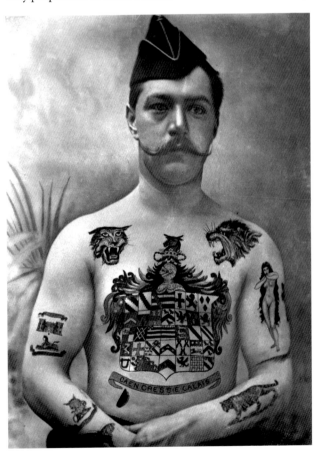

were superior to all of nature – a sentiment echoed loudly in the west by the Catholic Church, which decrees that animals have no souls and rejoices in the Christian creation story which states that God created animals solely for the benefit of man. According to Catholicism they have no claim to existence in their own right and are simply there to be used. The Chinese, rather more romantically, believed that the tiger had a soul, which in her last dying 'congealing glance' formed the waxy mineral amber. *Xuo-p'nk* is the Chinese word for both amber and the tiger's soul, its pronunciation and etymology identical. The basis of this mythology is unknown but it seems likely it is related to the beautiful amber colour of the tiger's penetrating eyes.

However, one of the first examples of the tiger being transformed into a servant of man is seen in Chinese bronze objects from at least as early as the sixth century BC, showing this

In this image from an 1810 album of Sir Charles D'Oyly, an Indian civil servant and artist, the elephant is composed of many animals, including the tiger, and symbolizes its rider's domination of the world.

magnificent creature, symbol of all that is free, with a collar on her neck. This indicates they were kept in captivity, and as another notable feline, the cheetah, has long been used in the east for hunting it seems likely that domestic tigers were kept for hunting antelope and horse and perhaps for doing battle. The latter may seem a strange concept but the Romans kept divisions of large, mastiff-like dogs to patrol the borders of their empire, and a creature more likely to induce fear in the enemy than the tiger, and to signal one's own regal might, is hard to imagine. Do these lines from the *Yi King* (*c.* 800-600 BC) support this theory?

> The King spread his war might
> He thundered and he raged
> Forward went his tiger slaves
> Fierce as ravening tigers

Perhaps, although another explanation could be that the king's warriors were dressed as tigers as the tiger is also the symbol of Chinese military might.

More conclusive evidence that tigers were used in hunting comes from the burial grounds of the Lower Capital of the Zhou Court, now known as Old Loyang. One large group of tombs from this site, dating to around 300 BC, were constructed from pottery tiles a massive two by five feet in dimension. The majority depict hunting scenes carried out in a lively flowing manner which embraces both the heraldic Chinese ceremonial style and the more naturalistic style of the nomadic peoples of northern China. Several depict tigers wearing collars and crucially one shows a tiger being held on a leash by her keepers. The tiger is clearly what used to be called *Felis tigris longipilis* or the Manchurian woolly tiger, a title which makes this massive long-haired predator, now reclassified as *Panthera tigris altaica*, seem

An early Chinese tomb tile from Old Loyang showing a tiger wearing a collar, perhaps for a leash.

almost cuddly.[2] Further evidence of this tradition, and its longevity, comes from the court of the Great Khan at Kublai, Cathay, in the fourteenth century, where Marco Polo states there were 'several great lions, larger than those of Babylon. They have very handsome coats, of beautiful colour, striped length wise with black red and white. They are trained to take wild boar, wild cattle, bears and wild asses, stags small deer and other small beasts.'

According to Pliny, the perhaps more pragmatic denizens of the Indian subcontinent harnessed the tiger's power by encouraging it to mate with their hunting bitches when on heat. Even the reputed progeny of these dog/tiger crosses were considered too fierce to handle and only the presumably more manageable third litter were reared.[3]

In the main, tigers avoided the animal holocausts of the Early Roman Empire (29 BC–AD 117), for transporting them from the East was an arduous undertaking and leopards and lions abounded locally. But, if available, they too were used for dispatching criminals and Christians: Petronius wrote enthusiastically 'the padding tiger is carried in a gilded palace, to drink human blood while the crowd applauds'.[4] However, despite being chosen for their ferocity and undergoing training by *bestiarii* at a dedicated school – Pompeian frescoes show a leopard attached to a bull to somewhat restrict its movements being trained to attack an unfortunate youth – many of the big cats refused to attack the prisoners tied to their stakes in the Roman arenas, and were so terrorized by the bloodthirsty yells and cries of the crowd that they ran cowering to the comparative safety of their cages. Usually only dire hunger brought success and 'sometimes this was pushed to such a point that the executioner rolled over and died at the feet of his victim'.[5]

Christian martyrdom at the paw of the tiger was glamorized by romantic European *fin de siècle* painters such as Briton Rivière (1840–1920). The reality was rather more tawdry. Wealthy Roman individuals, keen to display their wealth by conspicuous consumption, maintained large private menageries of trained lions, bears and, no doubt, tigers. Allowed the freedom of their masters' homes, they strolled around, disconcerting unwary visitors. The Emperor Elagabalus' quadrupeds were let into his sleeping guests' bedrooms by way of a prank.[6] But of course, with even the best-trained predators accidents did happen, and Roman law thoughtfully provided for compensation.

A second-century AD Roman mosaic of a tiger hunt, Antioch.

Briton Rivière,
A Roman Holiday,
1881, oil on
canvas.

Keeping collections of exotic and native animals has for thousands of years been seen as the ultimate status symbol because it is a hobby which can only be indulged by the extraordinarily wealthy. In modern times it is not so much associated with those in political power as those who dominate the global celebrity stage, such as Michael Jackson. In the past, particularly, the denizens of these menageries were destined not only to be admired in their pitiful cages but often to provide entertainment in the form of animal contests. In the West this is now outlawed and animal contests have gone underground but in Pakistan, for instance, it is completely acceptable. Where tigers are concerned, their opponent is usually the magnificent crescent-horned buffalo, a tradition that certainly dates back to the time of the great Mughal emperors and probably before. Akbar liked to pit trained buffalo against wild felines. The buffalo were ridden by hunters who forced their 910 kg steed to attack the tiger by catching her on its horns and tossing her so violently that she died. Abul Fazl, Akbar's biographer, declared 'It is impossible to describe the excitement . . . one does not know what to admire more, the courage of the rider or his ability to stay on the slippery back of the buffalo.'[7]

By Shah Jehan's reign (1627–65) things had escalated. Jehan would order an area of jungle to be encircled with high nets, so strong that it was simply impossible for a tiger to escape through them, and then would send through the only entrance a hundred fighting buffalo followed by him and his favourites in open howdahs on elephant back. The buffalo riders armed with broad swords advanced slowly in a half-moon formation until the tigers were sighted, then completely encircled them. Trapped, 'each tiger springs in the direction it sees best. When this spring takes place the man who is mounted on top jumps off with agility, and the buffaloes seize the tigers with their horns with great dexterity and shaking their heads tear them to pieces. If any of the tigers escape the horns or refuses to stir from its place, the king fires his gun and kills it . . .'.[8] The tiger's head was then covered with a leather bag and the royal seal affixed by a court official. She was carried to Shah Jehan's encampment, where the court official in charge of poisons chopped off her whiskers, which were later employed in court intrigues. Although we might choose to laugh at this seemingly naïve notion, in fact tiger whiskers are incredibly hard and when chopped into tiny, tiny fragments they rupture human intestines just as ground glass does.

There is something ultimately debasing for both killer and the killed when the victim has no chance of escape, no possibility of winning, but these kind of contests stir an elemental blood lust, a desire for death, destruction and degradation, which lies barely beneath humanity's civilized veneer, waiting for any opportunity to emerge. As animal engagements go, it is, however, hard to find one so sadistic and by its very viciousness so entirely illustrative of total and absolute power as this entertainment hosted by the governor of Saigon in the middle of the nineteenth century. A tiger 'was secured to a stake by a rope tied round his loins, about thirty yards long. The mouth of the unfortunate animal was sewn up, and his nails pulled out'. Forty-six elephants were then lined up to attack the tiger one by one. The first 'raised the tiger on his tusks to a considerable height, and threw him a distance of twenty feet'; even so the tiger sprang onto the elephant, who bolted from the arena leaving the tiger attached to his rope. The elephant driver bound with rope was dragged into the arena, where he was held face down and whipped with bamboo 'by a succession of executioners' acting on the governor's orders, until, insensible, he was dragged away. Meanwhile ten elephants one by one tossed the tiger until the falls finally killed it.[9] Still, as the English narrator of this edifying story confides, the people of Saigon 'have few public amusements, or sports or pastimes'.

Meanwhile, that paragon of virtue Queen Victoria was enjoying a fight between a tiger and bull held in Spain, where the bull was 'in the full vigour of health', while 'the spirit of the tiger was evidently subdued by a long imprisonment'. 'The tiger advanced a few steps then seeing the bull he suddenly placed himself in fighting attitude. The tiger made a spring with the intention of grasping the the bull with his claws, but the latter laid the tiger dead with one thrust of his horns.' Ninety thousand individuals attended this event and bets totalled 100,000 lire.[10] Of course, Victoria was only following tradition.

One of the first striped predators to reach a European menagerie was a tame tigress given to Louis XIV of France by the Moroccan ambassador.[11] As 'gentle as a bitch', she was stroked, adored and caressed by the queen and her ladies and was paraded around St Germain on a lead.[12] However, her status as a beloved pet did not save her from having to take part in interminable animal conflicts, which were now at the height of their popularity. As this particular tiger survived many conflicts

'Of the Tiger',
from Edward
Topsell's *History of
Four Footed Beasts*
(1607).

Of the *TIGER.*

perhaps these entertainments were more by way of gruesome
stage spectacle than actual fights to the death, like some of
the combats at the ancient Tower of London menagerie, now
Regent's Park Zoo. After all, tigers were rare and mysterious. In
the West at least they were hard to replace and no doubt their
long-term status-enhancing presence and, later, their worth as
fee-paying crowd-pullers was not to be underestimated.

The Tower of London menagerie evolved from three lions
given to Henry III (1216–1272) by the Holy Roman Emperor,
Frederick II, on the occasion of his marriage to Isabella, Henry's
sister. Taken from the Emperor's private zoo, the animal members of which all attended the magnificent marriage ceremony,
they tangibly demonstrated Frederick II's enormous power and
endowed Henry with tremendous prestige. On arriving in
London in 1235 the big cats were sent to the Tower, a prison and
a palace for both man and beast. By 1240 the original flesh-and -

blood gifts were dead and the Tower evolved into a dismal place with animals crammed higgledy piggledy into solid stone prisons arranged 'in the form of a half moon' with 'iron grates through which you look at them'. These dens were 3.7 m high and were divided in two horizontally, their occupants inhabiting the upper apartment in the day, the lower at night.[13] For the big cats the excruciating boredom and surely claustrophobic panic was relieved from time to time by being forced to engage in fights or being baited by fierce dogs to entertain the reigning monarch and the public, and in a variation on 'feeding time at the zoo' being thrown live spaniels as a toothsome snack. An early account of the menagerie tells that

> there is likewise a young Man Tyger, a mischievous beast; he'll heave anything at strangers that happen to be within his reach, but care is taken that he can get at nothing that will hurt. If you fling anything at him, you

'Combat at the Tower of London between a Lion, Tiger and Tigress', 1830, lithograph.

cannot hurt him; for he catches with great dexterity. He is but very young but by his motions when women approach him, he appears to be lecherous to a surprising degree.

Another commentator notes that tigers are 'very playful and leap a prodigious height, when like cats they are playing their gambols'.[14]

A children's book of 1741 reveals that the 'Lions, Tigers, Panthers and Leopards, are fed sheep's heads and plucks twice a day of which a lion eats four or five in a day; but Leopards, Panthers and Tigers, are much fonder of raw dogs-flesh', and that 'They drink as often as they please. Usually several times a day; each having a stone trough in his den.' The fortunate tiger recipients of this largesse were Will and Phillis, captured 'from the South Sea', who 'sport and play wantonly together', and their cub Dick.[15]

Such was the fascination with these exotic creatures that in 1764 even John Wesley, the founder of the Methodist Church, was unable to resist testing if the animals were moved by music, thus signalling that they possessed souls. Having a hired a flautist for the occasion, Wesley noted:

He began playing near four or five lions; only one of those rose up, came to the front of his den, and seemed to be all attention. Meantime, a tiger leaped over the lion's back, turned and ran under his belly, leaped over him again, and so to and fro incessantly.[16]

Until the advent of the Tower Menagerie, English artists had found it difficult to find live models for their representations of exotic animals, and the resulting images were unique combinations

'Fanny Howe, Whelp'd in the Tower', an etching of 1794.

Théodore Géricault, *Combat of a Lion and a Tiger*, early 19th century, watercolour drawing.

Three engravings after drawings by George Stubbs: 'Lateral View of a Tiger Skeleton', from his *A Comparative Anatomical Exposition of the Structure of the Human Body with that of a Tiger and a Common Fowl* (1817).

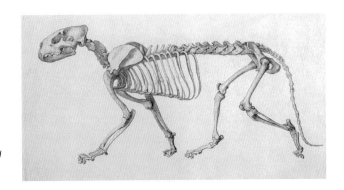

'Tiger: Lateral View, Partially Dissected', from his *Comparative Anatomical Exposition . . .* (1817).

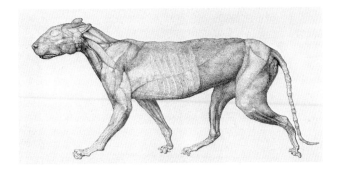

'Tiger: Lateral View, Skin Removed', from *A Comparative Anatomical Exposition* (1817).

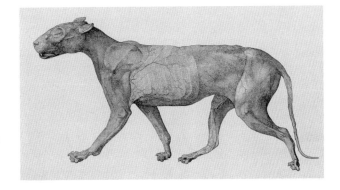

of the artist's imagination and descriptions provided by travellers who had glimpsed the fabled beasts.

They now had the genuine article available here and in other private menageries and the tigers and other creatures quickly became models for all the great masters. George Stubbs (1724–1806), a painter of flair and poetic imagination, one of the world's finest observers of nature, and one who felt true empathy with these fellow creatures, having obtained the body of a tiger to dissect, from 1802 until his death engaged himself on the superlative *A Comparative Anatomical Exposition of the Structure of the Human Body with that of a Tiger and a Common Fowl*.

William Blake (1757–1827), an esoteric visionary, was also far from immune to the extraordinary magnetism of the tiger, and repeatedly took the trip from his apartments in London's Lambeth district to the Tower to study the felines in their miserable brick cells, who were described by his contemporary Oliver Goldsmith as 'fierce and savage beyond measure'. The poem and painting of the tiger that resulted from Blake's visits have become his most famous works. *Songs of Innocence* and *Songs of Experience* were intended by Blake to illustrate the two contrary states of the human soul, the dichotomies that exist in every facet of life. The contrary poem to that on the tiger is 'The lamb', which is about a kindly and gentle god who likens himself to this sweet creature. Did this god make the 'dread' tiger too, and if so what does he represent? And what does 'dread' mean to Blake? In his time, the word meant reverenced as well as feared. When Blake asks what immortal hand dared make this creature burning so brightly in the forest night he is surely celebrating the wondrous power of the tiger, so incandescent that even an immortal would stand in awe of his creation. He saw beyond the tawdry state of her degradation because in capturing her image

'Tyger Tyger . . .', from William Blake's *Songs of Experience* (1794), a hand-coloured engraving.

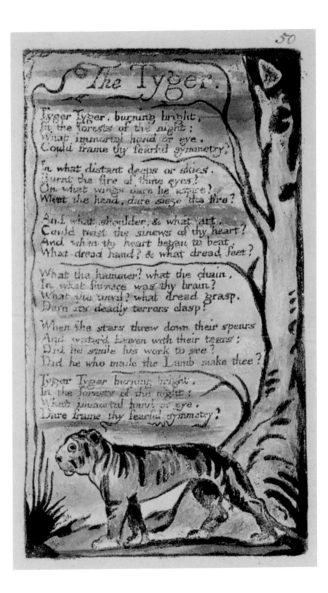

he created a creature so beguiling in aspect that it is hard not to imagine that he felt anything less than compassion for this living creature. But perhaps this is another expression of the contrary qualities that dwell within both man and beast. Whatever Blake really intended, the line 'Tyger, Tyger, burning bright' has itself been burnt into western consciousness and is celebrated still, as in the extraordinary pyrotechnic tiger created by Robert Bradford as the twentieth century drew to a close.

Most men and women of power contented themselves with living menageries. Augustus II, the Strong, of Saxony (1670–1733) went one further: exploiting the most costly and desirable substance of the age, he commissioned a life-size menagerie in Meissen porcelain copied from the creatures in his flesh and blood zoo. In one stroke he emphasized his fabulous wealth and impeccable taste, and demonstrated by owning creatures such as the tiger the reach of his awesome power and, further, his extensive knowledge of the animal kingdom through

Robert Bradford's 1997 pyrotechnic sculpture *Tyger Tyger.*

A caged tigress, c. 1910.

A Dresden porcelain tiger, c. 1730.

his ability to maintain his charges in robust health. In fact the exotics rarely survived long and on death were sent to the taxidermists prior to taking their place at his Dresden Zwinger palace, where a monumental display of stuffed creatures, feathers and bones was displayed. The eight porcelain tigers were a superb demonstration of technical skill and true artistic ability, but realistic tigers they were not. Instead, these felines modelled by Kirchner were plastic, possessing a soft, quizzical, anthropomorphic expression and a small lion's mane to express nobility and majesty. A Baroque expression of the age's attitude to animals, their portrayal's purpose was only to symbolize human values and ideas.

By the nineteenth century menageries were no longer the sole province of the powerful. They had become democratized, and travelling menageries owned by ordinary people entertained the masses. The new breed of entrepreneurs who ran these shows found that one of their biggest draws was the tiger, which

Tiger and tamer
in a French circus,
c. 1935.

The taxidermy
studio in the
Museum
d'Histoire
Naturelle de Paris,
1892.

caused the number of tigers in captivity to blossom exponentially. As the downtrodden and oppressed fought their way to equality they wanted to enjoy the things that had once been the province of the wealthy Their demand for menageries mirrors the desire of Indians who, after independence, saw slaughtering tigers as a democratic right which put them on a par with those who had once ruled them. This has led to extraordinary numbers of tigers being held in confinement, the majority in America. So much so that there are now around eight times as many of these top predators languishing in captivity as there are in the lands that are their birthright.

The menageries vied with one another to produce the most exotic captives. In England, in 1827, T. Shore's boasted a black tiger, 'the only one ever seen in this kingdom'. Mr Shore boldly offered a massive reward of £500 to 'any person who ever saw, in any other travelling menagerie A Black Tyger'. Wombwell's Menagerie was another extremely successful travelling show which in a neat status reversal was patronized by Queen Victoria herself. But tigers not only languished in menageries, they were frequently to be seen on the London stage, where they were cunningly woven into stories such as *The Forest Queen*, whose first night at the Garrick Theatre on Monday, 21 November 1831, was described as 'A new Eastern Tale of Enchantment' with 'REAL LIONS, TIGERS, ELEPHANTS, BOA CONSTRICTORS, PELICANS OF THE WILDERNESS, KANGAROOS MONKEYS AND MACKAWS WHICH ARE ENGAGED AT IMMENSE EXPENSE' and included 'Mahud on his state elephant for the diversion of a tiger hunt!!'[17]

The cat master and darling of the New York and London stage was the mid-nineteenth-century Isaac van Amburgh, a man whose career started when, drunk on wine, he was dared by friends to enter a big cats' den and amazingly survived. And so began a phenomenon that exemplifies the cruel way in which animals were treated, the stress they endured and the joy that audiences of this time felt when they saw nature on its knees and their dominion confirmed. The press dubbed him 'The Modern Androcles' and noted, as might be expected, 'the sentiments evinced by the animals towards him are of a mingled nature: displaying both fear and affection, in high degree'. Van Amburgh used a crowbar to control his felines and related to the press that when he first put his lions, tigers and leopards in a cage together (he specialized in putting a variety of predators together with their natural prey, such as a lamb, in a confined space), 'death to some of the combatants would inevitably ensue', had he not, club in hand, for the first time rushed into the cage, and by a deluge of blows awed the ferocious belligerents into subjugation. Not surprisingly from that hour on 'they seemed to have inspired a dread of their powerful opponent'.

In 1838 Van Amburgh took Drury Lane by storm in a 'Grand Chivalric Entertainment' called *Charlemagne* that endured for 115 performances. In one of the major scenes Charlemagne condemns a traitor to 'the tender mercy of certain forest radicals, lions, tiger, panthers and leopards who have recently been caught'. Needless to say it is Van Amburgh who subdues the wild creatures and makes the tiger 'a pillow'.[18] Queen Victoria was one of the many who attended the show and she requested that she might watch the edifying spectacle of the big cats being fed. Van Amburgh had already kept them without food for 36 hours when during the pre-feeding performance the lion and panther had 'simultaneously attacked the lamb [another cast member] on its being placed in their den; and they would evidently [have] made but a mouthful apiece of it, had not their almost superhuman master literally lashed them into the most abject and crouching submission'. When finally fed,

A typical Ringling Bros and Barnum & Bailey Circus poster.

the rolling of the tiger's eye, while he was devouring the massive lump of meat and bone clutched between his forepaws, seemed to posses the brilliancy and rapidity of lightning; and was only diverted by a sudden and tremendous spring by the lion, who . . . seized upon what was left of his neighbour's fare. The dash . . . was enough by its force and fury to shake the strongest nerves.

Queen Victoria, however, displayed the usual English stiff upper lip and 'deeply riveted, continued to gaze upon the novel and moving spectacle'.[19] But not everyone judged the level of their wild charges' frustration as accurately as Van Amburgh. Ellen 'Lion Queen' Bright, aged 17, Wombwell's brightest star attraction, on 20 November 1850 unwisely struck her tiger twice, at which the feline 'running upon its hind legs it seized her by the neck, she fell on her back, the tiger crouching over her. A large wound under the neck, and shock, produced death.'[20]

These shows were part of a burgeoning social democracy that believed, and continues to believe, that equality is defined by the individual's right to own as many possessions as they wish. Ironically this democratization has, in reality, not fostered equality but encouraged people to elevate their status and emphasize their difference from others through conspicuous consumption. And in America, where until the passing of the 1973 Federal Endangered Species Act anyone who wished to could buy lions and tigers from private zoos and mail order companies, many individuals turned to the time-honoured tradition of owning and, just as importantly, being seen to control and be adored by, top predators. Unsurprisingly many of the people who anticipated glorious social acclaim on receipt of their new purchase found the reality of big cat ownership both more expensive and much more arduous than anticipated. Although predators can be trained, it takes time and patience. Instead of training their 'pets' in the main their owners instead declawed them, castrated them and finally had their teeth pulled out before abandoning them in sorry condition – the fantasy that their big cat was just an adorable pussy cat which would bestow love on them was by then ashes.

Although top predators will superficially settle into their restricted lives and show affection for their keepers – just as humans who have been kidnapped finally long for their abductors in a sea of unremitting monotony – in reality these creatures constantly suffer from anxiety, frustration and generalized chronic stress, being unable to exercise their natural desire to flee from man, to reproduce and to hunt for their food. Wild animals, and predators in particular, have high levels of adrenaline production, which regulates the fight or flee response, and low levels of seratonin, which inhibits aggression. In domestic animals this balance is reversed. Only intensive selective

A dramatic entrance at the Shambala animal preserve in California.

breeding for creatures who are infinitesimally less fearful and aggressive to man or, to put it another way, fractionally tamer, over tens of generations, as has been done in Russia with wild foxes by Lyudmila Trut,[21] can alter hormonal levels to the degree which is necessary for wild animals to behave as domestic animals do, and not to feel stressed in the company of humans.

Tigers are intelligent animals, and placed in a situation of forced inactivity they are excruciatingly bored, intensely frustrated and edgy. They can hardly be blamed if they attack the hand that feeds them with dead meat and turns the key to their prison. The only surprise is that they didn't do it sooner. One person who rescued a large number of abandoned big cats in the USA was Tippi Hedren, star of Hitchcock's *The Birds* and *Marnie*, who with her husband spent many years filming *Roar!*, a passionate plea for the preservation of African wildlife. The rescued lions, leopards and tigers (curious plot adaptations managed to accommodate the tigers in the film) at one point numbered over 80 and shared Tippi's ranch Shambala, just 40 miles north of Los Angeles, and wandered free within its borders. They had plenty of social interaction, gambolled, played, attacked water sprinklers, and slept on Tippi's bed if they were so inclined. Tippi did not employ handlers who used fear to control her cats but instead spent time assessing their body language and, when filming, she and her husband set up scenes, let the cameras roll and recorded what happened. A *Times* review panned the plot but stated that the animals were 'superb, and shamelessly skilful in all the techniques of upstaging; there is an irresistible thrill in seeing an understanding between humans and animals that overturns centuries of preoccupations about relationships in nature'.

But even in such a benevolent human setting the realities of putting wild cats into domestic situations were poignantly evident. Although birth control was the order of the day at Shambala, it was thought that tigons, the progeny of a lion and a tiger, were sterile. Noelle, a tigon, was to prove them wrong when her days of passion with a tiger called Anton resulted in

Liger cubs – lion/tiger crosses – in Samsung Everland Safari Park, South Korea, 2004.

the birth of Nathaniel. Noelle had been used to the run of Shambala and sauntered in and out of 'the office', which opened on to a sand pit, perfect for young cubs to roam in safety. She now chose 'the office' to be her den and set about erasing every sign of human habitation and began to raise her cub as a wild animal.

> At first, different pieces of furniture – chairs, a waste basket, the typing table – seemed to annoy her, and we removed them, She then began to clear my desk with swipes of her paw, so I removed those objectionable things . . . Soon we had removed everything except two big filing cabinets . . . But Noelle finally turned one over, partially blocking her access to Nathaniel. Frantic she bit and clawed them, leaving punctures in the steel about the size of .45 calibre bullets.[22]

Naturally Noelle became possessive of her cub and resisted efforts to 'humanize' him. To prevent a possessive bond and to

The rare, almost legendary, white tiger.

'Akbar slays a tigress which attacked the royal entourage', an illustration by Basawan from the *Akbarnama*, 1590–95, opaque watercolour and gold on paper. This is the earliest-known representation of white tigers.

make taming Nathaniel easier, he was removed from Noelle after a few weeks. In the wild they would stay together for almost two years. Nathaniel screamed for three days while his mother, who could hear him, paced, paced, paced through the dark, long night.

The rarer the beast the greater the kudos of possession, and because of this the sublime white tiger has attracted the unwelcome attentions of man more than most. Astonishingly beautiful and magnetically alluring, with ice-blue eyes, thick creamy white fur shot through with dark chocolate-brown stripes and 600 lb of solid svelte muscle, she truly is an unforgettable sight. However, these tigers are not albinos or members of a subspecies; they are an anomaly, the result of a disadvantageous recessive gene. In the wild, the qualities humans admire so much are a liability. Glaringly obvious against dark jungle foliage and dappled shade, all the tiger's weapons of predatory stealth and ambush are lost, and natural selection ensures very few survive in the wild. As far as the author is aware, the last recorded individual was shot in Bihar, India, in 1958.[23]

In 1951, the former maharaja of Rewa's hunting party shot a tigress and three of her cubs. The fourth, a white cub, was finally lured into a tiny wooden cage. Freedom over, Mohan's domain became a room with an open courtyard in the maharaja's palace. A normal coloured tigress, Begum, was taken from her home in the forests to become Mohan's mate. Although they had three litters, none of the cubs was white. Finally Mohan was mated with his daughter, Radha, who bore him four white cubs. Virtually every white tiger in the world, with extremely rare out-breeding, is descended from this tiny gene pool. These unfortunate creatures are so inbred that they suffer from physical defects which include sway backs, twisted necks, cross-eyes, weak eyes, lumbar paralysis, shortened tendons in their forelegs and weakened and compromised immune systems

which make them prey to everything from pneumonia to infestation by the parasite trypanosomiasis.[24] Like all populations whose genetic diversity is compromised, a large percentage of white tiger cubs are stillborn, many matings do not produce offspring at all and there is also a very high rate of spontaneous miscarriage.

Not one of these tigers has ever tasted freedom, known the extent of their still awesome power, even reduced as it is, or padded through the dark velvet jungle night, and they never will. The only reason they exist at all is for entertainment, as a spectacle to be gawped at, for the ego gratification of their owners or, last but far from least, for their ability to make their owners huge sums of money. And this is so whether they are in Bristol Zoo, on stage at the Mirage Hotel in Las Vegas or enduring a never-ending life on the road performing for any of the circuses that the Hawthorn Corporation, the largest breeders of white tigers in the world, lease them to.

The Las Vegas magicians Siegfried and Roy cloak the existence of their white tiger tribe with the sanctity of 'conservation' and have founded a white tiger breeding programme with the Zoological Society of Cincinnati. This makes a complete mockery of real zoo conservation programmes, which seek to preserve genetic diversity, as well as those people who risk their lives to conserve the tiger in her own forest lands. White tigers are the compromised result of a feline eugenics program. White pots of gold – they are hard business dressed up as sentimental schmaltz, even if their owners do, as Siegfried and Roy appear to, have a real passion for them. Over 30 million people had paid to see Siegfried and Roy's show at the Mirage Hotel when, in October 2003, one white tiger, Montecore, put an end to the whole affair. Montecore was fascinated by a woman in the front row with a large and 'freakish' hairdo who was preparing to stroke the giant

American magicians Roy Horn and Siegfried Fischbacher with celebrities, January 2002.

feline. Roy attempted to make Montecore focus on his performance but the tiger responded by growling at him. Roy 'told him no and bopped him on the nose with his microphone'. Montecore grabbed Roy's sleeve in his mouth, Roy stumbled and fell back, a classic trigger for predatory behaviour, and Montecore went for the kill – or, according to Siegfried and Roy, picked Roy up to take him to the safety of backstage to protect him from from the ensuing chaos.[25] Whatever Montecore's motivation, Roy was very seriously injured.

William Philadelphia, an early twentieth-century big-cat trainer, puts the tiger's viewpoint succinctly:

> The wild beast is afraid not so much of any pain that may be inflicted upon him, but of some vague unknown power too great for him to understand or cope with. This is what gives the tamer control of his lions and tigers. It is not any personal magnetism or any inherent virtue not possessed by other men . . . it is merely that one particular man, by untiring patience has succeeded in making himself appear in the lion's eye as the one great and boundless force of the universe before which he must bow.[26]

Animals such as Montecore are unable to express themselves and it is this silence which allows the illusion that they are content living in their prisons, whether these are comfortable and well appointed, as certainly those run by Siegfried and Roy are, or miserable barred cages. If they speak out in frustration as Montecore did, against 'the boundless force of the universe', 'they are quickly made silent again, perhaps for good'.[27] And this holds whether they are chimps, lions, wolves or any other sentient being. Montecore, however, it must be emphasized has not apparently been punished, indeed he is roundly defended by Siegfried and Roy, and at the time of writing is presumed to be living his usual life with the rest of the menagerie. Siegfried and Roy have not resumed their show.

Meanwhile, also in October 2003, Antoine Yates, in a startling piece of synchronicity, was attempting to create 'a Garden of Eden' by living in harmony with an alligator and a Siberian-Bengal tiger in a fifth-floor apartment in Harlem, New York. This tiger also spoke by biting Yates's leg, and has since been transferred to Noah's Lost Ark in Berlin Centre, Ohio, which specializes in rescuing such unfortunates and lobbies strongly that wild animals should never be kept as pets.

The desire to keep big cats seems to transcend any degree of logic. In safety-obsessed Middle America the rationalization is, risibly, that tigers are 'safer' than if they were in their 'dangerous' natural habitat. Imprisonment has now magically turned into something which is *good* for tigers while freedom, which is every living creature's core aim, is *bad* for them. Elizabeth Marshall Thomas, an extremely influential American animal behaviourist, prolific writer and classical anthropologist, vigorously promotes this view, stating unequivocally that tigers positively enjoy circus life and performing tricks in the ring. No doubt they do, for the ring is a welcome change from their normal life, which Thomas enthusiastically describes thus: 'The owners live in small trailers and tigers live in travelling cages on wheels, each cage about twice the length of the tiger who inhabits it. Sometimes nothing better than a large tarp or the edge of a circus tent shelters these little groups of people and tigers just barely protecting them from wind sun & rain.'[28] Thomas sees in this condition a charming interdependence, a mutual endurance of hard times which engenders closeness and, putting herself in the tiger's place, she remarks how preferable this existence would be to living in anything but the finest of natural habitats. She also champions John

Japanese sliding door-panel with tiger; *c.* 1614, ink, colour and gold leaf on paper.

A tiger on a painted screen, drawn in ink on paper by Soga Shōhaku (1730–81).

Cuneo's Hawthorn Corporation, a dedicated commercial enterprise which breeds white tigers expressly for circuses in northern Illinois. For over two decades, Cuneo has constantly been cited for violations of animal welfare regulations by the United States Department of Agriculture (USDA), which include on 23 April 2002 being cited for failure to provide minimum space to 14 white tigers living in transport cages, a citation repeated in June 2002; failure to provide an adequate veterinary care programme;

144

A Korean Yi dynasty painting of a magpie and a tiger, 18th or 19th century.

providing mouldy food and feeding inedible food to tigers.[29] But hey! they're *safe!*

Humanity's increasing alienation from nature coupled with a desire to view animals as non-sentient beings, who exist only to be used by us, has resulted in the bulk of humanity refusing to acknowledge that wild animals belong in the wild. An early advocate for these much abused creatures was the lyric poet Ralph Hodgson (1871–1962), whose 'The Bells of Heaven' expresses a deep empathy for animals and a critical look at the human condition:

'Twould ring the bells of Heaven
The wildest peal for years
If Parson lost his senses
And people came to theirs
And he and they together
Knelt down with angry prayers
For tamed and shabby tigers
And dancing dogs and bears
And wretched, blind pit ponies,
And little hunted hares.

Other cultures, in other times, have dealt with the psychology of fear and the psychological desire to exert power and to tame nature in many different ways and, if some have at times used savage means, not all of them have sort to destroy and degrade all that is wild and magnificent of spirit.

That the tiger engenders fear when first seen is not surprising. To look into those great eyes, to feel intimately the power which throbs through every fibre of her being, is to feel awe and to understand one's own impotence when compared to an elemental force of nature. But there are many ways of controlling fear and taming the untamable, and one of these is a belief in the power of sympathetic magic. Rural women in Bengal populate their traditional *kanthas* – wraps and quilts made from scraps stitched together – with exquisite embroidery featuring the animals that surround them: the elephant, the chital deer and, of course, the tiger, who is usually part of a hunting scene, making him subject to the power of both the hunter and the embroiderer. This device gives confidence to the wearers when they walk along forest paths, for how could a creature in such thrall present a danger?

The Warlis, who live just north of Bombay, make depictions of their revered tiger god which have a benign, almost gentle, aspect to them, rendering the fearsome beast inoffensive and mild. Although the tiger god Vaghya is recognized as a wild, ferocious aspect of nature, the Warlis do not seek to kill his fleshly representative. Instead they propitiate him with sacrifices so he will not take their cattle or bite them and credit him with protecting their village, their homes and themselves, saying that 'all mature people' would remember his power and ask for his help if travelling to distant places.

Another way of neutralizing the tiger is to make her a figure of fun, an amusing but silly creature who is easily outwitted, and no culture has done this more successfully than the Korean, which has turned the tiger into a jovial household pet. Innumerable folk tales tell of a foolish tiger being cajoled, reasoned with and even hoodwinked, and countless paintings portray her in humorous and unthreatening ways. Predators, feline and canine, are always accompanied by members of the crow family, who, showing no fear of their powerful furred fellows, cheekily snatch leftovers from their kill and hover above them playing a kind of tag. Unsurprisingly, Koreans have frequently chosen this subject matter to illustrate the tiger's absurdity.

In the West, too, the tiger is now often depicted as a silly capering figure so harmless that she can be a magical friend to children. But although tamed, the tiger still retains sufficient aura of her once great power to make her an ideal emblem for foods such as Kellogg's Frosties, promoted as giving energy, vitality and health. Tony, who has fronted up the sugary breakfast cereal since 1952, now inhabits the consciousness of children in over 42 different countries. In the 1970s Mama Tiger emerged and in 1974, the Chinese Year of the Tiger, she gave birth to tigress cub Antoinette, and a dynasty was established. In England, however, there can be no more thoroughly tamed and utterly adored tiger than Tigger, Winnie the Pooh's dearest friend.

Tony the Tiger on the Kellogg's Frosties box-front.

Other peoples who live intimately with the tiger have created compassionate deities who control the forests and the movements of the tiger, listen to the prayers of their devotees and protect them from harm when they venture into the forest to harvest beeswax, honey or wood. In the Bengal Sundarbans, the only place in the world sufficently hostile and unpalatable to humanity that two or three hundred tigers can still continue in their primeval state, it is the lovely Banabibi. Encounters with the feline 'hero of the jungle' are inevitable, and when this happens, Muslims and Hindus together perform a ritual to the powerful but kind and generous Banabibi. Religious differences mean little in the face of tigers who hold the power of life-and-death. As a further safety precaution, woodcutters, who travel through the thick mangrove swamp in little open boats, also employ fakirs or *guinons* to select their collecting grounds so they may avoid encountering the amphibious predator.

If despite all these precautions a tiger emerges from the dark green glades, she is subdued with magic mantras:

Franz Marc, *The Tiger*, 1912, oil on canvas. Marc empathized with his subjects, striving to capture their essence, not their zoological reality.

Chalani: which drives the tiger to another area of the forest;
Jvalani: which makes the tiger's body itch and burn, causing her to feel uneasy and leave the area;
Khilani: which makes the tiger's jaws cramp preventing her from opening her fearsome mouth.

And that standard, all-purpose fallback incantation of magicians worldwide: *abracadabra*.

But the *guinon* can be overcome, for the cunning tiger sometimes attacks him and by putting her paw on his face, preventing him from uttering his charm. The denizens of the Sundarbans are, however, beginning to lose faith in the fakirs whose once glorious powers, they say, have dwindled. It seems reasonable to speculate that in the past these men had an intimate knowledge of the swamps and a naturalist's instinctive knowledge of the tiger which modern fakirs do not take the time to accumulate. Tigers tend to patrol the same beats, they have fairly specific territories, they are to a degree creatures of habit. A knowledge of this and the triggers that cause them to attack would surely be of wondrous help in protecting the woodcutters. Despite the fact that woodcutters have been killed by tigers – the nature of their work necessarily intruding upon the feline in a very direct way – they respect her. As Shri Bag, speaking in the 1960s, said, 'We pay our never failing regard to the deity Banabibi, but we do not hate the tiger, we rather appreciate its intelligence, valour and dignity. We really have awe and wonder for the tiger.'

5 Conservation

I pray, when a lion eats a man and a man eats an ox, why is
the ox made more for the man than the man for the lion?
Thomas Hobbes, 1641

By 1938, when the enthusiastic animal slaughterer Jim Corbett
wrote that 'the taking of a photograph gives far more pleasure
to the sportsman than the acquisition of a trophy' (something
he appears to have forgotten when he became the director of a
safari hunting company in Nairobi, Kenya), it signalled that
even dedicated hunters like himself were beginning to realize
that the supply of new victims was becoming severely limited.
Following in the footsteps of the naturalist Fred Champion,
the first photographer of tiger land, Corbett spent four months
of 1938 using a cine-camera to film tigers in daylight. The result
is a phenomenal and unique glimpse into the last moments of a
world that has now disappeared. Corbett located seven tigers
and lured them a few yards at a time over a period of months
to his 'jungle studio', an open ravine fifty yards wide, with a
tiny stream flowing down the centre of it, and flanked on either
side by dense tree and shrub. More vivid and curiously more
natural than slick contemporary documentaries, Corbett's eye
takes the viewer deep into the tigers' world. Sure-footedly they
pad to their bait, water sparkles, forest flower blooms hang
heavily, their scent being almost palpable; this is nature at its
most fertile, primitive and unsullied. Relaxed, the tigers' tails
flick lazily, they scratch their ears like charming domestic
cats and pose elegantly and unknowingly on a massive flat

rock, their great paws hanging over its edge, a monument to the past.

Photographing tigers is now as popular with those who visit India's reserves as hunting once was and, for many, the mentality is identical. Instead of looking at the environment as a whole and appreciating the wondrous intricacies of the forest ecosystems, admiring lush mango fruit trees, flying squirrels, mongoose and elephant alike with the eye of one who loves nature, these contemporary hunters spend their days in jeeps screaming around safari parks with only one object in view: to shoot the tiger. Almost everything else is lost to them. But to preserve the tiger without the complexity of her lands is to preserve something without substance.

There are so many problems besetting conservation not only of the tiger, which has its own unique set of problems, but of the entirety of the ecosystem in which it dwells, that it is hard to single out one more than another, but surely changing the consciousness of humanity, the deep-seated behaviours which dictate the way it has viewed the natural world for hundreds of years, is crucial to success. And one of the viewpoints that we need to shift to is that we are not separate from the rest of nature but are one part of an interdependent whole.

With the Enlightenment of the seventeenth century came the triumph of science, the victory of the rational and the provable. René Descartes (1596–1650), one of its most famous icons, added to the legitimacy of Christianity's view that animals were created solely to be used by man, by declaring that animals were unfeeling automata with no ability to acquire knowledge. These two mantras of the West set man far apart from the rest of nature and sanctioned psychological or physical cruelty, destruction of habitat and even extinction. Although archaeological evidence induced many Christians to abandon belief in their creation story, the assumption of use and inferiority was too deeply rooted in the Western psyche for mere fact to dispel it. And the mainstream scientific community and more recently global corporations find it extremely useful to manipulate these deep-seated cultural assumptions so that they can continue to, for instance, indulge in the excesses of vivisection, cut down virgin forests for paper, construct overland oil pipelines and, in India in particular, mine habitat. To this end, environmentalists, naturalists and those who empathize with animals and recognize that they are sentient have been derided. The concept that animals have some legitimate claim to the lands once their birthright is another anathema as it prevents 'development' and 'progress'.

Although environmentalists are gaining ground and the view that we are a part of nature, not apart from it, is beginning to be more accepted, those with vested financial interests are still in the ascendant virtually worldwide and it will take a mas-

Entire fresh tiger skin being used to decorate a *chuba* at Litang Horse Festival, Sichuan Province, China, August 2005.

sive effort to turn the tide. Recently, in May 2005, a further, and more serious crisis, which could push the tiger into extinction and threatens to be one of the biggest scandals in conservation history, was exposed in the world's press. The Environmental Investigation Agency revealed that 'the entire tiger population has been wiped out of Sariska Tiger Reserve, that possibly 18 known individuals have disappeared from Ranthambore Tiger Reserve, nine known breeding tigers from Panna Tiger Reserve, with a further 21 missing or unaccounted for.'[1] And this is only the news from high-profile reserves. If tigers can disappear from places such as these what hope is there for their survival in inaccessible reserves or unprotected forest land?

This scandal was so great, so all-encompassing, that India's prime minister Manmohan Singh has ordered an enquiry into what happened at Sariska, and a full and comprehensive census of tigers throughout India. The last census put their population at 3,624, which many working in the field consider to be a falsely inflated figure. If the carnage throughout India is anything like the scale shown in these northern reserves, it seems unlikely that even 1,500 of these magnificent, irreplaceable felines remain. Singh has also crucially leant his support to the establishment of a National Wildlife Crime Bureau and recognized the need for dedicated services to manage forests and wildlife. However, none of this will aid the protection of the forests unless those recruited are committed, professional enforcement officers and those in direct charge of the reserves are not open to bribery and are genuine, experienced conservationists and naturalists. Those in charge of the reserves and several government ministers admit that poaching is a simply an overwhelming problem. While the demand for tiger skins, bone and meat in China and Thailand is constant and clamouring, there will always be poaching. At root it is these markets that must be destroyed by altering the cultural attitude that applauds eating tiger meat as a source of strength and potency and using the bones to cure rheumatism. Unfortunately this will take at least a generation, the norm for cultural attitude change – and for the tiger that may be too late.

For the meantime, urgent action is necessary and cultural attitudes must also change in India. A task force established by the chief minister of Rajasthan, which includes environmentalist and naturalist Valmik Thapar, who has devoted his life to preserving the tiger, has already revealed that warnings from NGOs and local community leaders that tiger poaching was evident were ignored and that this is commonplace throughout Indian reserves. No one is prepared to take responsibility, fearing that they will be sacked or moved to another post or because the poaching is taking place with their compliance. The task force has already discovered poaching gangs in Sariska; one admitted killing 10 tigers out of a population of 18. Arrests have been made and a city dealer, Sansar Chand, unmasked, but this is the tip of an international iceberg.

In Panna, villagers inside the reserve's core area admit to poaching in massive groups of 25 to 50 people, and not only tigers but the deer which are their prey and crucial to their survival.[2] How could this happen on a properly managed reserve that possesses many lookout posts? The answer is, of course, that it couldn't, and the story of Panna, where I have studied tigers, illustrates many of the problems that beset tiger conservation as a whole. Panna, in Madhya Pradesh, was one of the success stories of conservation. When Shyamendra Singh first came there in 1986 and established his Ken River Lodge on the banks of the devastatingly beautiful Ken River, he began seriously to lobby on behalf of the park. At that time there were many more villages in the park than there are now; there was cattle grazing, cattle camps, and so much movement that all the animals in the area were disturbed, and so, in the main, both kept a critical distance and became nocturnal. The herbivores on which the tiger depended were doing poorly because they were in direct competition with the cattle and the few resident tigers were forced to move well beyond the park boundaries to find better quality jungle.

The forest guards naturally find themselves in constant conflict with the villagers, as their aims are so disparate. For the guards the results of this conflict can be devastating, because if a villager makes a complaint against a guard, he has to fight the case himself, with his own funds and without backing. This situation has changed slightly as the forest department now has a welfare fund, so at least the man's family does not starve (I write that in the literal not metaphorical sense), but taking money from the fund is at the director's discretion – a system clearly open to abuse if the director is in any way involved with the villagers' activities. This is one small example of the administrative problems which run through all conservation in India and which urgently need to be addressed.

During the 1990s Panna was fortunate in having a dedicated, honest Forest Officer, Mr Choudhury, who was prepared to spend time in the field and whose enthusiasm spread through the ranks, allowing Panna and its wildlife to flourish. (In 2005, scandalously, senior management at Sariska were not even posted on site and did not supervise its patrols.) Mr Choudhury, combined with extra funds, cattle being removed, provision of walkie-talkies and more patrol vehicles, meant that the quality of the forest itself improved, and herbivores began to increase, allowing the tiger population, which is directly dependent upon them to also increase. Success brings its own problems, however. As Panna can only support around 40 tigers, this means that

Diamond-mining in Panna Tiger Reserve, India, 2000.

A tiger in the Panna Reserve.

sub-adult males need to stake out their own territories away from the resident dominant males, and to do this they are forced to leave the reserve. As there is no buffer zone round Panna this brings the tigers into direct conflict with the villagers, particularly as the tigers will take prime milking cattle. The villagers then usually poison the cattle carcass. Another tiger is dead.

So, for the tiger and many other animals the question of territory and space is paramount. In the whole of the Indian sub-continent there are now only four areas – Khana, Bandipur, Nagarholie and the Sundarbans – that provide sufficient contiguous forest to allow tigers to live in the way 1.5 million years of evolution has equipped them to do, and even these are hardly adequate. Three hundred tigers or, indeed, bears, pandas, panthers, spread in one area sufficient for their needs are much more likely to survive and increase in numbers than 300 tigers split into 10 groups of 30 each in one tenth of the area, which is essentially the situation in most reserves today. In small groups there is constant inbreeding, genetic diversity is compromised and, even if there are no specific genetic diseases such as sway back, the overall vigour of the population is greatly reduced. Small groups are much more prone to being wiped out by disease. Similarly if large groups are poached, there is some chance of regeneration. Take away the few breeding tigers from a population of 30 and the whole group may simply be unable to reproduce itself. The problem of genetic diversity can to some degree be mediated by providing forest corridors between reserves so tigers can establish territories in other areas and add the genes to the pool. Shyamendra Singh is lobbying for funds to buy land to act as corridors from Panna to sanctuaries 350 km away in Utter Pradesh, even if these corridors are only 1 km wide. As things stand, tigers are inclined to use railway tracks to travel from nearer reserves such as Bandavgarh.

Dr Raghu Chandawat set up a research project to monitor the tigers in Panna using telemetry, and made a beautiful film following the progress of one tiger matriarch. Sadly, the way the film was presented made it appear that all the good work in the park had been due to Dr Chandawat's efforts, which was certainly not the case, and created bad feeling. Chandawat's research among other things identified a need for more chital – one of the tiger's favourite prey animals in Panna, and to this end he asked the park management to cut down saplings so they had more open land, but in his opinion management took things too far. Litigation ensued in the Indian High Court, the end result of which is that now reserves must not deviate from their annual management plans. This has advantages as it certainly helps prevent abuses but it also means management cannot respond quickly to changing situations.

Chandawat controversially used telemetry in the park, but in real terms simply monitoring where tigers are and if they are active or resting tells us very little and, worse, almost turns them 'into abstractions, mere points on a map and activity graphs; it reveals little about them as living beings with daily problems and aspirations';[3] and there are grave dangers involved in darting and anaesthetizing creatures such as tigers. Dosages may be wrong, there may be problems when they come to as they are extraordinarily vulnerable, and there may be adverse reactions.

I asked Dr Chandawat if he thought that the spread of population in India, which has left only small fragmented pockets for the tiger and intrudes further on their tiny territories every day, was a major factor mitigating against the tiger's survival. He replied 'we can save the tiger if we have the will'. Maybe, but increasingly only in controlled environments where humanity must constantly intervene and that is not wild animals living wild lives.

Ranthambore, an extremely high-profile reserve in Rajasthan, illustrates perfectly what happens as tiger sanctuaries become popular tourist destinations, isolated pockets in an ever-burgeoning sea of humanity. Valmik Thapar, one of the tiger's foremost protectors, has struggled for years to make Ranthambore a real sanctuary for the tiger, somewhere a tigress may find the seclusion she needs to rear her cubs, where their prey is bountiful and their lives natural. He has documented their lives and taken on the overwhelming bureaucracy and at times corruption of the system but even he is overwhelmed. Writing in 1992, he commented:

> The supposed success of Ranthambore Project Tiger Reserve has attracted visitors from all over the world . . . but do any of these people take a day off from looking for tigers in order to see the outside of the park, to sit in a village and gain some insights into the attitudes of the people? No . . .

Further, he writes:

> But even the concerned observer who comes to watch the show is protected from the truth. Although there are nearly 300 kilometres of roads in the park visitors are only permitted on certain specified routes which make up less than $1/3$ of the total. They do not see the fringe and buffer areas of the forest. These other roads are misused by tractors and camel carts for collecting large and illegal quantities of wood. If these roads were closed and wood could only be taken away by the head load much of this despoliation would stop.[4]

In 2004 the situation had not changed in Ranthambore, and this is also true in reserves such as Khana. One of the reasons given for not taking tourists into these areas is to give the tigers and other animals somewhere that is theirs alone but though this may have been the original reason, now it is also to make sure tourists do not see these degraded areas and cause an outcry. But would things change? Perhaps, but the tourists themselves are helping destroy the tigers. Their numbers are soaring, increasing in the past decade from 36,808 to 67,981 a year and, as Govind Sagar Bhardwaj, the head of Ranthambore, says, 'politically influential hotel owners' are endangering the national park's future. 'Big hotels, supported by influential politicians, have a short-term view and keep demanding access for more safari vehicles to ferry growing numbers of tourists to see the tigers.' The park simply cannot cope with the number of visitors it receives and those with political connections have been allowed to build luxury resorts in eco-sensitive zones, further worsening matters. The tigers need peace; in Ranthambore they are constantly upset and harried. What chance for the small number, not even perhaps 20, who still survive in May 2005?[5]

I believe the only real hope of the tiger surviving through the next century and living as she did before the days of the Raj, the rape of the forests and the unbridled lust for tiger skin, tiger bone and tiger penis, is to preserve, untouched, those parts of the Sundarbans (a coastal area in northeast India and neighbouring Bangladesh at the mouth of the Ganges) which have not yet been destroyed. The measure of success in conservation is not how many tourists see tigers but the preservation of a healthy, genetically diverse population. This last wild outpost, originally known as Baghratatimandal – which probably meant tiger temple – before its steady degradation into a more commercial environment, was described, in even the nineteenth century, as an 'ideal stretch out abounding in morasses and swamps where the Carnivora could find their secure shelters',[6] an almost impenetrable maze of silt-loaded islands surrounded by waterways which flood 70 per cent of the land every single day. Water-loving, the tigers can swim from island to island, distances of even eight miles presenting them with no problems.[7] Sundarbans' tigers dine on crabs and fish and have even adapted to drinking salt water. The tiger is so versatile, so intelligent, so flexible, but she cannot survive without her lands, and now the mangroves on which the whole ecosystem is dependent are being chopped down for charcoal and the swamps, like mangrove swamps worldwide, are being lost to prawn farming. Nylon nets are constantly dragged down the riverbanks in order to collect the ironically named tiger prawn seeds. This destroys the mangrove seedlings that are necessary for the constant regeneration of the environment as well as destroying many fish species and the seed varieties which sustain them.[8] S. Mukherjee, deputy field director of Sundarbans Tiger Reserve, said, 'This is the most serious problem threatening the region. Though we are trying hard to regulate this practice, in reality the situation has gone beyond control and is damaging the entire estuarine ecosystem of the area.'[9] Lack of fish has its own knock-on effect by beginning to endanger the survival of the crocodiles. As the ecosystem's food chain breaks down more and more animals will be affected. The final result is as yet unknowable, but it is certain it will not be beneficial for the creatures that once thrived in this marvellous place.

Next time you see those giant tiger prawns basking on ice in the local fish department of your supermarket or offered with a spicy dip in your local Thai restaurant, remember where they came from and what effect you are having on the world's wildlife by encouraging their production.

The indigenous peoples of the Sundarbans have always collected wood, but the amounts were not sufficient to harm the overall ecosystem. Now, according to Radhika Ranjan Pramanik, Communist Party of India (Marxist) Member of Parliament from the Sundarbans, there is a major racket being run in the Sundarbans by timber merchants, who bribe forest officers and workers and collect as much timber as they wish. Timber from the forests of India is taken to make picture frames, cheap hardwood floors and cheap furniture for a Western society obsessed with throwaway objects and 'value for money'. By buying Forest Stewardship Council (FSC) wood and using re-cycled timbers, we can all help preserve the habitat of the tiger and other creatures worldwide.

Poaching the tiger and her prey the deer has always been rife in this area and is no doubt accelerating rapidly if the horrors of northern India are representative of the big business that poaching is today. It is chilling to consider that even 150 years ago the Sundarbans were rich with wildlife: the one-horned Indian rhino, the Javan rhino, wild buffaloes and river dolphins flourished. All are now extinct in this area. Now a major tourist company, Sahara India Pariwar Group, wants to 'develop' 305 hectares of land, covering it with five-star floating hotels, high-speed boat-houses, hovercraft facilities, helipads, a golf course, a floating casino perhaps, and although Sahara's intent is unclear, fish processing and a breeding facility for crocodiles and tigers, the latter being particularly pernicious. There is already a sub-stantial captive tiger population in India; it is impossible to introduce any of them into the wild as they have not been taught the hunting skills essential for their survival – something which takes over two years in the wild – and it seems more than possi-ble some of these animals will find their way into the tiger parts trade in Asia, thus further stimulating demand and poaching.

Sahara cloak their activities under the name of eco-tourism, which the World Conservation Union defines as

> Environmentally responsible travel and visitation to relatively undisturbed areas in order to enjoy, study and appreciate nature (and any accompanying cultural features – both past and present) that promotes conservation, has low visitor impact, and provides for beneficially active socio-economic involvement of local populations.

Sahara's proposals if accepted by the government of Bengal will destroy the Sundarbans, the shrimp fisheries it sustains, 'and the livelihood it gives to thousands of people with firewood, timber, medicines, honey and other natural products',[10] besides making it considerably easier for poachers to penetrate the Sundarbans and decimate the last remaining wildlife. It will also pollute the environment; floodlights will alter the behaviour of the animals and allow them no peace, and the development of beaches will reduce the buffering effect current vegetation provides against the sea, something that in the wake of the tsunami of December 2004 is hardly trivial.

The tiger is already extinct in Bali, Java, Korea and China and the Caspian, is on the brink of extinction in Sumatra and retains only a tiny paw-hold across Thailand, Vietnam, Cambodia and eastern Russia. Is she now to be deprived of the only place in the world where a few hundred of her kind can live in peace? India was once a land of limitless forests. The boughs of great neem trees moved gently in response to tropical breezes, massive teak trees grew in the mountains of the Western Ghats, sweet-smelling conifers covered the Himalayas. The British turned these fecund areas, which for generations had provided the people of the subcontinent with everything they needed, into commercial properties to provide them with wood for their railway sleepers and to run their trains, to make their ships and to make paper to feed an ever-burgeoning bureaucracy. Entire forests were felled and replaced with plantations of cotton and indigo and non-native species, all of which had a devastating effect on the ecology and the fragile water tables on which all life depended. The problem exploded after independence and the assassination of Mahatma Gandhi. Greedy foresters felled entire areas, which were then over-grazed by cattle and goats and suffered from soil erosion, meaning they could never be regenerated. The homes of tigers, elephants, deer and people were lost forever. In the 1970s even more forests were sacrificed so that consumers might have plywood, rubber, eucalyptus, tea and ever more coffee.

Villagers once led sustainable lives. The forests of Ranthambore used to provide lacquer from the chila tree, allowing them to make beautiful jewellery; now the only forest is within Ranthambore tiger reserve and thus forbidden. Millions of people who lived in harmony with their natural surroundings, who understood the balance of the forests and their importance to life, now have no forests to inhabit. Strangers in a strange land, they have been forced to live in ways they find uncongenial. Some leave and go to cities such as Delhi, where often they end up begging; many have been forced into agrarian economies, which further degrades and removes natural habitat; many have to resort to poaching, which ranges from killing tigers to taking fragrant sandalwood, a semi-parasitic tree which is almost impossible to grow commercially and is now virtually wiped out of India; others daily deplete the forest reserves of wood for cooking.

Many people, though clearly not all, prefer to live in harmony with nature and want the forests to flourish as they once did. They want schools to teach their children about the environment around them and how to live fruitfully within it, and to a large

A vendor of amulets and medicines made from tiger body-parts – including claws, c. 1920.

degree it is on these people that the survival of the tiger, and ultimately nature, depends.

For the tiger to survive, first and foremost, the Sundarbans must be protected from development. Forests need to be expanded by judicious planting so that people who live in harmony with nature and wish to continue doing so can. Cultural attitudes to the consumption of tiger parts must be changed and poachers and parts traders punished harshly. Real eco-tourism must be adopted and we, the consumers, must think very carefully of the real cost of our 'cheap' material objects and our desire to consume, which is driven by multibillion-dollar companies and their mega-advertising campaigns.

It is the right of nature to survive that must be defended, not the right to consume and exploit. The natural heritage that is our children's right must be saved so a humanity now divorced from nature and increasingly alienated may again find peace.

An adult male tiger on a forest track, Kanha National Park, India.

Timeline of the Tiger

30 MILLION BC	2 MILLION BC	10,000 BC
Proailurus lemanensis, the first cat, although with rather more teeth than today's felines. Remains have been discovered in France	*Panthera* separates into various species: *Panthera tigris* (tiger), *Panthera leo* (lion), *Panthera pardus* (leopard)	The eight geographical *Panther tigris* subspecies (Caspian, Siberian, Southern Chinese, Indian Chinese, Bengal, Sumatran, Javan and Balinese) begin to evolve

500 BC	220–206 BC	*c.* 300 AD	1119–25
First evidence of feng shui in China. In her form as the White Tiger of the West, the striped feline balances the energy of the Azure Dragon of the East	Earliest known text of the *I Ching* or Book of Changes. The White Tiger and the Azure Dragon representing male and female energies combine in Hexagram number 63	Hua Tuo develops medical shadow boxing, the forerunner of Tai Chi and Kung Fu. It is based on the movements of five creatures: the deer, the monkey, the bear, the crane and the tiger	*The Water Margin*, one of the greatest books in Chinese fiction, concerns rural bandits who fight ruling-class oppression. In a famous scene, Wu Sung fights and bests a tiger 

early 1900s	1944	1947
Esso Norway first uses the tiger logo to advertise its petrol/gasoline; in time it goes global, making the Esso/Exxon tiger one of the world's most iconic and successful advertising campaigns ever 	Publication of *The Man-Eaters of Kumaon*, swashbuckling – and reputedly real-life – tales recounted by Jim Corbett, one of the British Raj's chief tiger slaughterers	Independence and Indian democracy exponentially accelerates the slaughter of India's remaining tigers

3500 BC	2637 BC	c. 500 BC

People living by the River Amur in east Russia create tiger petroglyphs on basalt rocks, the earliest known images of the striped feline

Emperor Huangdi introduces the lunar calender on which Chinese astrology is based. It has a 60-year cycle composed of five simple cycles, each 12 years in length. The tiger represents the third year of each cycle

In his incarnation as Prince Mahasattva, the Buddha uses the tiger to illustrate what Buddhists consider to be the greatest of all virtues, compassion

1560	c. 1600	c. 1793	1900

Portuguese ecclesiastics in Malacca gravely excommunicate a number of supernatural weretigers while in their human form

Mughal emperor Jahangir keeps pet tigers in a stupendous menagerie and gives us the first intimate natural history reports of the supreme predator

Tipu Sultan, ruler of Mysore, India, and an implacable enemy of the British, commissions 'Tipu's Tiger', a life-size automaton comprising a growling tiger devouring a British soldier

All eight tiger subspecies still extant at this time, but over the next few decades, the Caspian, the Southern Chinese, the Javan and the Balinese will become extinct

1969	1972	2005

Thanks to tireless campaigning by Kailish Sankhala, the tiger is at last placed on the Red Data book of endangered species

The tiger replaces the lion as India's national animal

Massive poaching decimates the tiger population in the reserves of Panna, Sariska and Ranthambore. The hotel group Sahara plans to develop part of the Sundarbans, the tiger's last truly wild retreat.

The tiger's destiny is again on the line – and this time it may really be her death knell

References

1 EVOLUTION AND NATURAL HISTORY

1 Alan Turner and Mauricio Antón, *The Big Cats and their Fossil Relatives* (New York, 1997).

2 Sandra Herrington, 'Subspecies and the conservation of Panther tigris: Preserving genetic heterogeneity' in R. L. Tilson and U. S. Seal, eds, *Tigers of the World: The Biology, Biopolitics, Management and Conservation of an Endangered Species* (Park Ridge, NJ, 1987), pp. 512–60.

3 Colbert and Hooijer, 'Pleistocene Mammals from China', *Bulletin of the American Museum of Natural History*, CII (1953).

4 Mary Linley Taylor, *The Tiger's Claw: The Life-story of East Asia's Mighty Hunter* (1956).

5 Richard Perry Cassell, *The World of the Tiger* (1964).

6 Shekhar Kolipakor, in conversation with the author.

7 Kailish Sankhala, *Tiger!: The Story of the Indian Tiger* (London, 1978).

8 Pliny, *Natural History*, VIII.

9 Frances Eden, *Tigers, Durbars and Kings: Fanny Eden's Indian Journals 1837–8*, ed. Janet Dunbar (London, 1988), from her original diaries, Oriental and India Office Collections, British Library, London.

10 Sankhala, *Tiger!*

11 Conversation with Shyamendra Singh, naturalist and conservationist, Panna.

12 S. H. Prater, *The Book of Indian Animals* (Oxford, 1998 [1948]).

13 Sankhala, *Tiger!*

14 Patrick Hanley, *Tiger Trails in Assam* (1961).

15 Prater, *Indian Animals*.

2 EARTHLY PASSIONS AND SPIRITUAL BALANCES

1 Frequently heard in conversation in Rajasthan by the author.

2 W. Perceval Yetts, *The Cull Chinese Bronzes* (London, 1939).

3 Stephen Skinner, *The Living Earth Manual of Feng Shui* (London and Boston, 1989).

4 See J.J.M. de Groot, *Chinese Geomancy*, ed. Derek Walters (London, 1989).

5 Skinner, *Living Earth Manual of Feng Shui*.

6 *The Taoist Classics: Collected Translations of Thomas Cleary* (Boston, 2003), vol. I.

7 R. H. van Gulik, *Sexual Life in Ancient China* (Leiden, 1974).

8 J. Rawson, *Western Zhou Ritual Bronzes from the Arthur M. Sackler Collections* (New York, 1990), vol. II.

9 Valmik Thapar, *The Tiger's Destiny* (London, 1992).

10 *Independent*, 9 May, 2004.

11 *Independent*, 9 May, 2004.

12 Environmental Investigation Agency, *Thailand's Tiger Economy* (2001).

13 Email to the author from Emily Bone at Pfizer, 14 May, 2004.

14 Wendy Doniger O'Flaherty, *Siva: The Erotic Ascetic* (Oxford, 1973).

15 A. Hiltebeitel, 'The Indus Valley "Proto-Siva," Reexamined through Reflections on the Goddess, the Buffalo, and Symbolism of Vahanas', *Anthropos*, 73 (1978), pp. 767–97.

16 Ghee is clarified butter, much used in Indian cookery.

17 William George Archer, *Bazaar Paintings of Calcutta: The Style of Kalighat* (London, 1953).

18 Yashodhara Dalmia, *The Painted World of the Warlis* (New Delhi, 1988).

19 Seen by the author. The photograph was also for sale in their Mirror Mirror department.

20 Kailish Sankhala, *Tiger!: The Story of the Indian Tiger* (London, 1978).

3 THE POWER OF IMAGE AND THE STRENGTH OF REALITY

1 Edward T. Bennett, *The Tower Menagerie* (1829).
2 Kailish Sankhala, *Tiger!: The Story of the Indian Tiger* (London, 1978), p. 135.
3 Sir George Maxwell, *In Malay Forests* (1907).
4 P. Boomgaard, *Frontiers of Fear* (New Haven, CT, and London, 2001).
5 Maxwell, *In Malay Forests*.
6 *Harivamsa (Vishnu Parva)*, ch. 16.
7 Valmik Thapar, *The Tiger's Destiny* (London, 1992).
8 S. H. Prater, *The Book of Indian Animals* (Oxford, 1998 [1948]).
9 Boomgaard, *Frontiers of Fear*.
10 Thapar, *Tiger's Destiny*.
11 www.mangalore.com
12 William Crooke, *Religion and Folklore of Northern India* (London, 1896).
13 *The Tiger Rugs of Tibet*, ed. Mimi Lipton (London, 2000).
14 Alexei Okladnikov, *Art of the Amur: Ancient Art of the Russian Far East* (New York and Leningrad, 1981).
15 Mircea Eliade, *Shamanism: Archaic Techniques of Ecstasy*, trans. W. R. Trask (Princeton, NJ, 1970).
16 Related in the *Kuo Yu*, 400 BC, but of more ancient origin.
17 W. C. White, *Tombs of Old Lo-Yang* (Shanghai, 1934).
18 *The Chinese Classics*, vol. V, trans. James Legge (Oxford, 1895), p. 293.
19 K. C. Chang, *Art, Myth and Ritual: The Path to Political Authority in Ancient China* (1983).
20 K. R. van Kooij, *Worship of the Goddess according to the 'Kalikapurana'* (Leiden, 1972).
21 Nelson Wu, *Chinese and Indian Architecture* (New York, 1963).
22 Shang period graves, e.g. at Xibeigang, Anyang, Henan province.
23 William Watson, *Cultural Frontiers in Ancient East Asia* (Edinburgh, 1971).
24 W. Perceval Yetts, *The Cull Chinese Bronzes* (London, 1939).
25 *Korean Cultural Heritage* (2002), vol. II, p. 212; Jane Portal, *Korea:*

Art and Archaeology (London, 2000).

26 Arthur Wellesley to the court of directors, January 1800.

27 Henry Willis, in Mildred Archer, *Tipoo's Tiger* (London, 1959).

28 Fillingham Collection of Cuttings, British Library, London 1889.

29 www.esso.be/Corporate/About/History/Corp_A_H_Tiger.asp

4 THE PSYCHOLOGY OF FEAR: THE TIGER TAMED,
THE TIGER DEGRADED

1 John Lockwood Kipling, *Beast and Man in India* (1891).

2 W. C. White, *Tombs of Old Lo-Yang* (Shanghai, 1934).

3 Pliny, *Natural History*, VIII, LXI, 147–50.

4 Petronius, *Satyricon*, 119, 14, writing during Nero's reign (AD 54–68).

5 George Jennison, *Animals for Show and Pleasure in Ancient Rome* (Manchester, 1937).

6 Cited in Jennison, *Animals for Show*.

7 Abul Fazl (Abu 'l-Fadl 'Allami), *Ain-i-Akbari* (Eng. trans. Calcutta, 1873–94).

8 Niccolao Manucci (a Venetian traveller who lived at Shah Jehan's court for many years); see *Mogul India*, trans. and ed. W. Irvine (London, 1900).

9 Miss Corner and Anon., *China; Pictorial, Descriptive, and Historical with Some Account of Java and the Burmese, Siam and Anam* (London, 1853), p. 329.

10 *The Times*, 25 May 1849, Court News. Another such event in Spain is reported in *The Times*, 26 July 1904.

11 D. Rybot, *It Began Before Noah* (London, 1972).

12 P. Belon, *L'histoire de la nature des oiseaux* (Paris, 1955), p. 191; Marquis de Sources, *Mémoires* (Paris, 1882), vol. I, p. 77.

13 David Henry, *An Historical Description of the Tower of London and its Curiosities* (London, 1757).

14 Thomas Boreman, *Curiosities in the Tower of London*, 2 vols (London, 1741), p. 75.

15 Boreman, *Curiosities in the Tower of London*, p. 44.

16 Daniel Hahn, *The Tower Menagerie* (London 2003), p. 2.

17 Fillingham Collection of Cuttings, 1889.

18 *New York Herald*, 23 November 1838, condensed from the *London Standard*.

19 Isaac van Amburgh, *An Illustrated History and Full and Accurate Description of the Wild Beasts and Other Interesting Specimens of Nature, contained in the Grand Caravan of Van Amburgh & Co.* (New York, 1846).

20 Fillingham Collection of Cuttings, 1889.

21 Lyudmila N. Trut, 'Early Canid Domestication: The Farm-Fox Experiment', *American Scientist*, LXXXVII/2 (March–April 1999).

22 Tippi Hedren, *The Cats of Shambala* (London, 1985).

23 Kailish Sankhala, *Tiger!: The Story of the Indian Tiger* (London, 1978), p. 90. He examined the Maharaja's hunting records himself.

24 For white tiger inbreeding in zoos, see A. K. Roychoudhury and K. S. Sankhala, 'Inbreeding in White Tigers', *Proceedings of the Indian Academy of Science*, LXXXVIII (1979), pp. 311–23.

25 www.eonline.com, 14 October 2003.

26 Cited in Cleaveland Moffett, 'Wild Beasts and their Keepers: How the Animals in a Menagerie are Tamed, Trained and Cared for', *McClure's Magazine* (May 1984), p. 556.

27 Nigel Rothfels, *Savages and Beasts* (Baltimore, 2002), p. 12.

28 Elizabeth Marshall Thomas, *The Tribe of Tiger* (New York, 1994).

29 www.kenglade.com for Spirit, the Southwest Airlines magazine.

5 CONSERVATION

1 www.eia-international.org: 'The third tiger crisis', 4 April 2005.

2 Jay Mazoomdaar in the *Indian Express*, 6 March 2005.

3 George B. Schaller, *The Last Panda* (Chicago, 1993).

4 Valmik Thapar, *The Tiger's Destiny* (London, 1992).

5 Times News Network, Thursday, 4 March 2004.

6 Tushar K. Niyogi, *Aspects of Folk Cults in South Bengal* (Calcutta, 1987).

7 O'Malley, writing in 1914 in the *Bengal District Gazetteer*, noted that 'a stray tiger was not long ago found at the mouth of

Rasulpur river, in the Midnapur district, which has swam across from Sagar Island, the breadth of the river being about 8 miles'.

8 A survey conducted in 1994 by the S.D. Marine Biological Research Institute, 24 Parganas (South) revealed that on an average in the process of collecting 519 prawn seeds, at least 5,103.25 gm of other seed varieties that sustain different categories of fish are destroyed.

9 *Frontline*, (published at Chennai), 17 November 1995.

10 Environmental Investigation Agency Sundarbans briefing, 17 March 2004.

Bibliography

Allami, Abul Al Fazl Ibn Mubarak, *The Ain i Akbari*, trans. H. S. Jarret (Calcutta 1891)

Ali, Salim, 'The Moghul Emperors of India as Naturalists and Sportsmen', *Journal of Bombay Natural History Society*, XXXI/4 (1927)

Amburgh, Isaac Van, *An Illustrated History and Full and Accurate Description of the Wild Beasts and Other Interesting Specimens of Nature, contained in the Grand Caravan of Van Amburgh & Co.* (New York, 1846)

Badoux, D. M., *Fossil Mammals from Two Fissure Deposits at Punang, Java* (Utrecht, 1959)

Baker, Sir Samuel W., *Wild Beasts and Their Ways* (London and New York, 1890)

Bannerman, Helen, *The Story of Little Black Sambo* (London, 1899)

Belon, P., *L'Histoire de la Nature des Oiseaux* (Paris, 1955)

Benn, Francis Brentano, *Big Cats* (London, 1949)

Bennett, Edward T., *The Tower Menagerie* (London, 1829, 1830)

Bernier, François, *Travels in the Mogul Empire*, trans. Irving Brooke (London, 1826)

Blurton, Richard T., *Hindu Art* (London, 1992)

Boomgaard, P., *Frontiers of Fear: Tigers and People in the Malay World, 1800–1950* (New Haven, CT, and London, 2001)

Bunker, Emma, *Nomadic Art of the Eastern Eurasian Steppes* (New York, 2002)

Cassell, Richard Perry, *The World of the Tiger* (London, 1964)

Chang, K., *Art, Myth and Ritual* (Cambridge, MA, 1983)

Choudhury, Ranabir Ray, ed., *Calcutta a Hundred Years Ago* (Bombay, 1987)

Cleary, Thomas, trans., *The Taoist Classics*, (Boston, MA, 2003), vol. I

Colbert and Hooijer, 'Pleistocene Mammals from China', *Bulletin of the American Museum of Natural History*, CII (1953)

Corbett, Jim, *The Man-Eaters of Kumaon* (Oxford, 1944)

Corner, Miss, and Anon., *China Pictorial, Descriptive, Historical* (London, 1853)

Courtney, N., *The Tiger, Symbol of Freedom* (London, 1980)

Crooke, W., *Folklore of Northern India* (London, 1896), vol. II

Dalmia, Yashodhara, *The Painted World of the Warlis* (New Delhi, 1988)

Devi, Ganga, *Tradition and Expression in Mithila Painting* (Ahmedabad, 1997)

Eden, Fanny, *Tigers, Durbars and Kings: Indian Journals, 1837–8*, ed. Janet Dunbar (London, 1988)

Endicott, Kirk Michael, *Batek Negrito Religion* (Oxford, 1979)

Fergusson, James, *Cave Temples of India* (1880)

'Fossil Carnivora of India', *Pal. Indica* n.s. XVIII (1932), 232

Geyer, Johann, *Inside a Menagerie* (Leipzig, 1835)

Gittleman J. L., S. M. Funk, D. Macdonald and R. K. Wayne, eds, *Carnivore Conservation* (Cambridge, 2001)

Gulik, R. H. van, *Sexual Life in Ancient China* (Leiden, 1974)

Hanley, Patrick, *Tiger Trails in Assam* (London, 1961)

Hedren, Tippi, *The Cats of Shambala* (London, 1985)

Holme, Bryan, *Advertising: Reflections of a Century* (London, 1982)

Jahangir, N., *Memoirs*, trans. A. Rogers and H. Beveridge (London, 1909)

Jennison, G., *Animals for Show and Pleasure in Ancient Rome* (Manchester, 1937)

Kipling, J. L., *Beast and Man in India* (London, 1891)

Kipling, Rudyard, *The Jungle Book* (London, 1975)

Kircher, Athanasius, *China Illustrata* (Amsterdam, 1667)

Kock, Deiter, 'Historical Record of a Tiger in Iraq', *Zoology in the Middle East*, IV (1990)

Kooij, F. R. van, *Worship of the Goddess according to the Kalikapurana*, part I (Leiden, 1972)

Korean Cultural Heritage (Korea, 2002), vol. II

Kurten, Bijorn, *On Evolution and Fossil Mammals* (New York, 1988)

Lau, Theodora, *The Handbook of Chinese Horoscopes* (London, 1996)

Lipton, Mimi, *The Tiger Rugs of Tibet* (London, 1988)

Loewe, Michael, and Edward L. Shaughnessy, *Cambridge History of Ancient China* (Cambridge, 1999)

Manucci, Niccolo, *Memoirs of the Mogul Court*, ed. Michael Edwardes (London, 1957)

Maxwell, Sir George, *In Malay Forests* (London 1907)

McCune, Shannon, *The Arts of Korea* (Rutland, VT, and Tokyo, 1962)

Moffett Cleaveland 'Wild Beasts and Their Keepers: How the Animals in a Menagerie are Tamed, Trained and Cared For', *McClures Magazine* (May 1984), p. 556

Nath, B., 'Animals of Prehistoric India and their Affinities with those of the Western Asiatic', *Records of the Indian Museum*, 59/4 (1966), pp. 335–67

Niyogi, Tushar K., *Aspects of Folk Cults in South Bengal* (Anthropological Survey of India, 1987)

O'Flaherty, Wendy Doniger, *Siva, the Erotic Ascetic* (Oxford, 1981)

Okladnikov, Alexei, *Art of the Amur* (New York and Leningrad, 1981)

Platter, Thomas, and Horatio Busino, *The Journals of Two Travellers in Elizabethan and Early Stuart England*, ed. Peter Razzel (London, 1995)

Pliny, *Natural History*, vol. III, books VIII–IX, trans. H. Rackham (London, 1967)

Polo, Marco, *The Travels of Marco Polo*, ed. Ronald Latham (London, 1958)

Portal, Jane, *Korea: Art and Archaeology* (London, 2000)

Prater, S. H., *The Book of Indian Animals* (Calcutta, 1998)

Purchas, Samuel, *Hakluytus Posthumus, or Purchas his Pilgrimes* (London, 1625)

Rawson, J., *Western Zhou Ritual Bronzes from the Arthur M. Sackler Collection* (Cambridge, MA, 1990), vol II

Rothfels, N., *Savages and Beasts* (Baltimore, MD, and London, 2002)

Roy, Asim, *The Islamic Synchronistic Heritage in Bengal* (Princeton, NJ, 1983)

Sankhala, Kailash, *Tiger!* (London, 1978)

Schafer Edward, *The Golden Peaches of Samarkand* (Berkeley, CA, 1963)

Schaller, W. B, *The Last Panda* (Chicago, 1994)

—, *The Deer and the Tiger: A Study of Wildlife in India* (Chicago, 1967)

Singh, Billy Arjan, *Tiger Haven* (New Delhi, 1999)

Skinner, Stephen, *The Living Earth Manual of Feng Shui* (London, 1982)

Sourches, Marquis de, *Mémoires* (Paris, 1882), vol. I

Sunquist, M. and F., *Wild Cats of the World* (Chicago, 2002)

Taylor, Mary Linley, *Chain of Amber* (Lewes, 1992)

Thapar, Valmik, *The Tiger's Destiny* (London, 1992)

—, *Wild Tigers of Ranthambore* (New Delhi and Oxford, 2001)

Thomas, Elizabeth Marshall, *The Tribe of Tiger Thomas* (London, 1994)

Tilson, R. L., and U. S. Seal, eds, *Tigers of the World* (Noyes, Minneapolis, 1987)

Toynbee, J.M.C., *Animals in Roman Art and Life* (London, 1973)

Turner, Alan and Mauricio Anton, *The Big Cats and Their Fossil Relatives* (New York, 1997)

Waley, Arthur, trans., *The Book of Songs* (London, 1937)

White, Bishop W. C., *Tombs of Old Lo-Yang* (Shanghai, 1934)

—, *Tomb Tile Pictures of Ancient China* (Toronto, 1939)

Williams, C.A.S., *Outline of Chinese Symbolism and Art Motives* (Shanghai, 1941)

Wilson, E. O., *Biophilia* (Cambridge, MA, and London, 2003)

Yetts, W. P., ed., *The Cull Chinese Bronzes* (London, 1939)

Zi, Ying, and Weng Yi, *Shaolin Kung Fu* (Hong Kong, 1981)

Associations and Websites

TIGER TRUST

Its mission is to save the tiger and preserve its natural habitat.
206 Rakeshdeep
11 Commercial Complex
Gulmohar Enclave
New Delhi 110049, India
phone: 011 651 67 70
fax: 91 11 686 5212
email: info@adventure-india.com
www.fontayne.com/tigertrust/release4.html

TRAVEL OPERATORS FOR TIGERS

If you are going to visit the land of the tiger, use a travel operator
who is a member. This is a collective campaign by UK and international tour operators to South Asia to advocate and help fund a
more sustainable wilderness experience that is capable of support-
ing wildlife, wilderness and host communities more effectively.
www.toftiger.org

DISCOVERY INITIATIVES

The Travel House, 51 Castle Street, Cirencester, Gloucestershire
GL7 1QD, UK
tel: (00 44) 01285 643333
fax: (0044) 01285 885888
email: enquiry@discoveryinitiatives.com

GLOBAL TIGER PATROL

Founded in 1989, GTP is a conservation agency prioritizing protection of the tiger in the field. If the tiger becomes extinct in the wild, most experts agree that it is extremely doubtful whether it can ever be reintroduced. In addition, GTP is a founding partner in 21st Century Tiger, a wild tiger conservation alliance with the Zoological Society of London.
www.globaltigerpatrol.co.uk

THE DAVID SHEPHERD WILDLIFE FOUNDATION

Funds innovative, long-term projects in Africa and Asia to achieve real results for the survival of species in their wild habitats while benefiting local communities who share those environments.
www.davidshepherd.org/index2.shtml

ENVIRONMENTAL INVESTIGATION AGENCY:

The EIA exposes illegal trade in skins, in body parts and in timber, and strives in every way possible to preserve the few wild animals left in the world and just as importantly their habitat from the depredations of poachers, dealers and of course those who consume these illegal products.
www.eia-international.org/

EIA LONDON

62/63 Upper Street, London, England N1 0NY UK
tel: 020 7354 7960
fax: 020 7354 7961
email ukinfo@eia-international.org

EIA USA

PO Box 53343, Washington, DC 20009, USA
tel: 202 483 6621
fax: 202 986 8626
email usinfo@eia-international.org

Acknowledgements

There are many people who have contributed to this book in their different ways and given of their valuable time. I would like to thank my series editor Jonathan Burt for his vision and understanding; my publisher, Michael Leaman, for producing books of value and worth; Deepraj Singh for generously letting me use images from his personal collection and for his unfailing hospitality to me in India; Shekhar Kolipakar for giving me wondrous insights into the wildlife of India; Shyamendra Singh for letting me share in his deep knowledge of tiger behaviour at Panna; Graham Hutt, Curator of Chinese Collections at the British Library, London, for making the inscrutable scrutable; Richard Blurton of the British Museum, London, for sharing his knowledge of Hindu art with me; the director of the Craft Museum in New Delhi for her invaluable assistance; Tim Jeal and Rupert Sheldrake for giving their precious time when I needed references; Julian Mathews, director of Discovery Initiatives, for arranging a truly wondrous wildlife trip to India for me; the staff of the London Library; and the staffs of Science Two South and the Oriental and India Office Collections at the British Library, London, for their unfailing courtesy and helpfulness in locating books and documents; and many others far too numerous to mention.

Photo Acknowledgements

The author and publishers wish to express their thanks to the below sources of illustrative material and/or permission to reproduce it. (Some sources uncredited in the captions for reasons of brevity are also given below.)

Photo © ADAGP, Paris and DACS, London 2006: p. 30; illustration from Mauricio Antón and Alan Turner, *The Big Cats and their Fossil Relatives* (Columbia University Press, 1997), by permission of the artist (Mauricio Antón): p. 10; photo courtesy of the artist (Robert Bradford): p. 127; photos courtesy of the author: pp. 49, 54, 57, 84, 85, 86, 87, 97; British Library, London (photos British Library Picture Library): pp. 40 (Royal 12 C. XIX, f.28), 45 (shelfmark 15113.e.6), 65 (OIOC photo 447/3 [59]), 76 foot (Wenshang 15201.a.1), 77 (YP. 2004.d.217), 88 (Add. Or. 3565; Archer Collection), 100 (Or. 6245, f.33), 113 (Add. Or. 4303); British Museum, London (photos © The Trustees of the British Museum): pp. 50 (1940.0713.051), 58 top (Museum no. P&EE OA290m), 66, 81 (1955.10-8.095), 98 (1990.11-13.02); Chiba City Museum of Art: p. 144; Clive Museum, Powis Castle, Welshpool: p. 102 (photo Erik Pelham/© National Trust Photo Library, 68146); © Salvador Dalí, Gala-Salvador Dalí Foundation, DACS, London: p. 62; Dinodia Picture Agency: p. 136 (RAA-15141); photos Enviromental Investigation Agency (© Robin Hamilton): pp. 23 (photo Robin Hamilton), 25 (photo Joanna Van Gruisen), 28 (photo Michael Vickers), 38 (photo Robin Hamilton), 48 (photo Faith Doherty), 153 (photo Belinda Wright), 157 top (photo Peter Richardson); photos Guildhall Library, Corporation of

Index